# INVOCATIONS

# INVOCATIONS

## Calling Forth The Light That Heals

*JACOB GLASS*

Writers Club Press
San Jose  New York  Lincoln  Shanghai

Invocations
Calling Forth The Light That Heals

Writers Club Press
an imprint of iUniverse.com, Inc.

For information address:
iUniverse.com, Inc.
620 North 48th Street, Suite 201
Lincoln, NE 68504-3467
www.iuniverse.com

ISBN: 0-595-14025-4

Printed in the United States of America

*Tom and Norma Belle Glass & Susie Lear*
*The Divine Mother*
*Spencer Garbett*

# Contents

# *Preface*

In the rainy winter of 1996, I was living in a damp and windowless basement studio apartment in San Francisco, California. I lovingly referred to my home as "The Batcave." I'd moved to Northern California 6 months earlier thinking that I would be able to lecture on spirituality as I had in Southern California, but that the city would attract a larger group of people. By January, I realized that although I loved the city, I was running out of time to make a go of it. Each week I was driving 300 miles from San Francisco to Santa Barbara to lecture to a group of 100 or so students. I was getting tired of the weekly drive and was waking up every morning lonely and very depressed. It seems I did not have the comfort of my own teaching.

Often, while in Santa Barbara, I would stay at a friend's home overnight. One afternoon as we were watching some local talk show, I was babbling on about how offensive I found the people on the panel. My friend said to me rather offhandedly, "You know, you're going to become bitter old man."

I felt as though ice water had been thrown in my face. I thought I'd been hiding my unhappiness, but obviously it was showing more than I thought. It was so humiliating to think that as someone who spoke about the power of love, I was not expressing much love in my own life. God was trying to tell me something. I realized that I had to make a change as quickly as possible or my attitude would poison my whole life.

The very next morning, I sat down and wrote the Daily Affirmative Prayer which is the first prayer in this book. You see, in spite of the fact that I had all kinds of experience and knowledge at my fingertips, in spite of the fact that I actually taught principles of love and healing, I still did not have a way of accessing that information in a powerful way on a consistent daily basis.

I had faith and belief, but I was disconnected from what those beliefs were, and so they were rendered powerless in my own life. I had goals and a mission, but without a connection to my spirituality my goals just made me more anxious and upset.

Now I was on a mission to turn myself around and get back on track. I put the Daily Prayer into my journal/appointment book and every morning, as I was having my coffee, I read that prayer. Reading it centered and calmed me in a profound way. After reading my prayer, I would write a few pages in my journal. As time went on, I incorporated my mission statement and goals into the process, but now my goals were part of the prayer and I was able to release the notion that I had to go out and force something to happen.

My life began to change immediately. I began to see things differently. Things started to fall into place in so many ways. Sometimes, I didn't even need to, so much as, make a phone call. Other times, I would gain an insight into something that I needed to do in order to make a change. Often, I would find renewed courage or inspiration to do something I'd been putting off for a long time. Sometimes, I would realize that I no longer even wanted what I had originally thought I wanted. It was like a daily mini-workshop that was actually fun and easy.

However, the greatest change is that I began to wake up happily looking forward to the new day. Soon thereafter, I received a phone call from a friend offering me a fantastic bright one bedroom apartment in Los Angeles surrounded by flowers and trees, at half the rent I was paying. I was able to get a computer and fax machine for my business, moved my lectures to a beautiful new venue and began making new friends; all things that I'd been praying about and had written in my personal prayer.

After a while, I shared the prayers and exercises with my students and was amazed to see their lives change as quickly as mine had, often dramatically. One woman told me she used the Daily Prayer to lower her blood pressure in the mornings. Another woman shared that she was using the prayers at a women's prison she worked for and, one young man said it was the only thing that he was able to read during a long hospital stay while recovering from a serious illness.

You do not have to suffer or be tormented by your own thoughts, or by the situations that are in your life. There is a way out that is loving and peaceful. You deserve a life that works. That is God's will for you. Together we can invoke the power of the divine and invite God into the situations of our lives.

I believe that these prayers and exercises can be of help to you on your daily walk. I am so pleased to be able to share them with you now. They continue to ground and uplift me in wonderful ways. This book is not a book of superstitious magic spells. It is not a replacement for any other spiritual practices you may already have, but rather is a wonderful addition regardless of your spiritual background. Just try it and see. My process and journey continues to unfold daily. I believe yours will too.

**NOTE:**

Although the chapter titles are followed by biblical quotes, and the vocabulary may seem to be Christian, this book is not intended for any particular religious group. I believe that there is truth and beauty in many different spiritual and religious traditions and honor whatever path you are on today. I am not a bible scholar and I use the bible as I use the sacred texts of many other religions, as a source of wisdom and healing. I am a seeker and student of divine truth and have found God in some of the most unlikely places. I am not trying to convince, convert or judge anyone. Many people have resistance to the bible because of the hateful ways that some people have used the bible to beat up on others. Let's not let that stop us from gaining the comfort that can be found there if we look closely.

# *Acknowledgements*

Many thanks to: Diane Meyer-Simon for her unfailing support—if not for her I'd probably have had to give up lecturing long ago, Marianne Williamson for always taking me to a higher level than I would have gone for on my own, Reverends Terry Cole-Whittaker and Sandy Scott for introducing me to the principles which changed my life, Kimberly Kirberger for her amazing encouragement and support, Jenny Bent for believing in me, Zan Gaudioso for calming me down and making me laugh, Jeannie Parkman for listening, Jenniffer Franks for friendship and for often saving the day, John Fahr for helping to edit my endless thoughts, Denise "Queenie" Longley for her constant generosity and friendship, Karen Bilger for being my first captive audience, Lori and Bernie Sandler for all their support and Jackie Sandler for my wonderful home, Mary Ruth Huffer for giving me the courage and assistance to start speaking publicly, Lori Newman and Bill Bolt for boundless dedication to showing up, Susie Leite for inspiring me by her willingness and beautiful meditations, Heath & Robert London for the laughs and my first trip to New York, Diane Dickinson for reminding me to have faith, Reverend Judy at Unity Church for giving me a chance, Crystal and Barbara at Victoria Hall, Tom Nelson for the incredible pictures, my little angel Marianne Orsua, Fannie Flagg, Colleen Casey, Larry Melby, David Kessler, Laurel Lucas, Chris Tucker, Yolanda Lebarton, Joannie Laine, Jaye Taylor, Jackie Eberhardt for being interested, Oprah Winfrey, Maya Angelou, Lynn Ianni, Bruce Munger for listening with compassion,

Omar, the Santa Barbara Tuesday group, my prayer partner John Mullican and the LA Monday night prayer group.

# *Introduction*

"You're the reason he'll never amount to anything! Of course the other kids don't want him around. He doesn't even dress like the other boys. You'll be taking care of him the rest of his life."

The words stung me as they filtered through the wall between my parents bedroom and my own. I wasn't supposed to be able to hear the accusations my mother hurled at my father, but angry words often carry over a greater distance than we realize.

I pushed the pillows over my head and scrunched down under the cover, deeper and deeper into darkness where it was safe and quiet. Well, not exactly quiet. The words rang out in my ears over and over again, louder and louder. Words that roared through my stomach like a runaway train. My whole body vibrating before going into shutdown.

I thought, "Why can't everyone leave me alone? I hate this town. I hate feeling this way. What's wrong with me? Why can't anyone love me? Why can't I do anything right? I have to get away from here and find someplace where I won't be hurt anymore. Someplace where I'll fit in and people will love me."

Yet long after I had left that house and the greenery of rural Pennsylvania, I would still hear those words and so many others haunting me as I went from town to town, person to person. It seemed that I couldn't outrun them no matter how hard I tried.

My mother was right, I didn't fit in anywhere. What I hadn't anticipated when I left, was that twenty years later, I would still be hearing those agonizing words, "Never amount to anything. Different. Failure. Quitter."

As a teenager the voice brought pain, but as an adult, the voice took on a particularly ugly and vicious tone that was often unbearable. It had become unbearable because now the voice was my own.

I'd spent most of my youth escaping into fantasy. My Catholic school upbringing equated suffering with sainthood and so it was easy for me to slip into a dreamworld where my persecution was merely proof of my holiness. I foolishly told myself that if I didn't fit in it was because I was different in the way that all truly special people are different. I was too skinny and afraid to participate in sports and too cripplingly shy to do much else. I was certain that I was the only person who felt so alone. Many times I would go out for evening walks and try to see in the front windows of the neighbors homes as I passed by, thinking that somehow I would get a glimpse, some clue of whatever I thought normal must look like. I knew it didn't look like me.

I became an expert at hiding in plain sight. Being noticed was painful. Being noticed usually brought not only verbal abuse, but many times, physical violence. Expressing any emotion, particularly anger, brought almost immediate pain. School was a place where I would be hit, spat on, humiliated and beaten up. Even teachers were not beyond ridiculing me and one even pulled my hair until my scalp bled. I would try to keep quiet in any unfamiliar situation. I didn't want anyone to see me or hear my voice. Often, I found that when I spoke to people in public they couldn't hear me because I was speaking so softly. Yet in spite of it all, I desperately wanted someone to notice what was good in me.

I learned to keep secrets from my family. It was too humiliating to let them know how horrible things were. How could I tell them that I was tormented daily, called names and ridiculed? I didn't want them to be dis-appointed or more worried than they already were. The truth is, I was afraid that maybe I *never would amount to anything*. Maybe other people were right. Maybe I was a freak and a nothing. Besides, I knew there was nothing they could do to change things. I saw first hand the way this world responds to anyone who is different in any way. If I didn't even feel safe to tell my own mother about my smallest problems, how in the world could I tell her that I hated my life?

By the time I reached the age of 23, I had moved to San Diego, California and began feel a little better about myself. Yet, I was still far from happy. I was having problems in all of my relationships and in every area of my life. As I looked around, I noticed that most of my friends were as messed up as I was. It wasn't a matter of what their particular situation was, that was just a smokescreen. I began to notice that a lot of people had the same critical voice in their heads that I had in mine. It told them that they were worthless or that other people were worthless. It held them back in crucial areas of creativity and expression. It victimized them as it victimized me. We all had different ways of keeping the voice down, drinking, drugs, food, sex, overworking, anything but face those horrible words.

There was so much I wanted to achieve and experience, yet I felt helpless to change my life. I had a deep faith in God, but no faith in myself. It wasn't enough anymore just to pray that things would get better. There had to be a better way. I had begun to beg God for help.

Then, in the late summer of 1983 after months of depression and unanswered prayers, I met my first spiritual teacher. She was a woman minister, named Terry Cole-Whittaker, who had a church in San Diego. She said that I could actively seek to change my life by first changing the nature of my thinking. When she talked about God, it was the God I'd believed in and known as a child. This God loved me unconditionally and wasn't angry at me. This was the God I remembered and knew in my heart. I began to feel differently. I began to experience my real feelings more. Something was happening. She taught me how to pray in a way I never had before, a way that made sense and gave me immediate relief and peace. She said that by changing my thinking I could change my life. She was right.

After a few years, I moved to Los Angeles where I studied with Marianne Williamson and Louise Hay. I read books by Deepak Chopra, Stephen Covey, Ernest Holmes, Joseph Campbell, Jean Houston and, I studied the Tao. As I studied more and more I came to realize that most of my problems were inside my own head. Ultimately, my suffering was the result of how I perceived everything that happened in my world. In fact, I began noticing how much of my time was spent actually tormenting myself with my own thoughts. For years I had been thinking that the problem was the situation or the people in my life. Now it was becoming clear that I found myself confronting the same emotional turmoil no matter who the people or what the situation. It reminded me of that horror movie where the babysitter has been plagued all night by menacing phonecalls. The police trace the calls and finally tell her, "The calls are coming from inside the house!"

The process of my growth and learning has been very gradual and filled with many mistakes. I found that it takes a lot of effort to get to effortless living. My heart has been broken many times. I've suffered greatly every time I have strayed from the spiritual truths that I have learned. I've been a very stubborn student at times, not willing to let go of "my way" until it was just too painful to hold on. Yet, I have found that God's grace is given me the very second that I let go of my control.

I still make mistakes but, they are not so far reaching anymore. I don't hang on as tightly as I once did. I realize now when I am stuck in my fearful thinking. I realize when I am tormenting myself with my own negative inner-voice and I seek the divine help that restores me to sanity. Taking responsibility for my own life, for my own thoughts and feelings, has been a very important tool in creating a joyful life of deeper meaning.

It is many years later now and although I can't say that I am never afraid or upset, I can say that I am happy in a way that is deeper than the external kind of happiness I dreamed of as a young boy. As simple as the principles of successful living are, it hasn't been easy, yet it has been worth every minute. I have had to work consciously every day to reprogram my mind from the thoughts of fear and lack to the divine thoughts of love. Sometimes I make it. Sometimes I don't. But, every day is another chance to do my best.

I now lecture to large groups of people in Southern California on the same principles my teachers have taught me. I've lectured to and counseled everyone from Hollywood celebrities to secretaries and ex-convicts. My own interpretation of spiritual principles is not for everyone. There are those who find me too offensive or controversial because of my language or the topics I choose or even the way I dress. Ultimately, none of these things matter to me. My goal is to make available the same message that others have so generously passed on to me. I have learned that a teacher is not someone who saves you from your problems. A teacher is someone who holds the light while you dig yourself out from under the cave-in of your own fearful thinking. Every time I have been down on my knees asking God to guide me, I have always been sent the messenger whom I could most easily understand. Dear Reader, if you understand what I am writing, then I am writing this for you.

*Jacob Glass*

# Chapter One

## What Is Prayer?

*"Ask, and it shall be given you; seek, and ye shall find; knock, and it shall be opened unto you: For every one that asketh receiveth; and he that seeketh findeth; and to him that knocketh it shall be opened."*

Matthew 7:7-8

My earliest memory of praying is in the bedroom I shared with my parents in the attic of my childhood home in rural Pennsylvania. From my parents bed, which was across the room from mine, my mother would listen to make sure I got it right as I said, "Now I lay me down to sleep, I pray the Lord my soul to keep, if I should die before I wake, I pray the Lord my soul to take." It scared me a bit to think that it was possible that I might die in my sleep.

Back then I thought God was someone "up there" looking down on me, watching and deciding who lived and who died. I suppose my prayers were more like bargaining than communing with the Divine. My motivation had more to do with guilt and fear than a deep love for God. I definitely believed in an Old Testament kind of God; angry and judgmental. In retrospect, it's easy to recognize that feelings of fear and guilt do not lead to closeness nor open honest communication.

Until my mid-twenties my prayers consisted mostly of either begging God to get me out of trouble I'd gotten myself into or asking to be saved from some anxiety-provoking future event. Having more to do with superstition than faith, I was treating God like a lucky penny.

As my own understanding of the spiritual principles of life has changed, so has the nature of my prayers. The most important aspect of my prayers now is the request that God's will be done. I think of it as the safety clause of all prayers. It keeps me from putting my self-initiated plans before the plans of God. It guarantees my ultimate happiness even if the outcome of the circumstance does not fit my particular preferences or pictures.

But for me personally, just the phrase "God's will be done" is not enough to bring me peace all the time. I have to ask myself, do I believe that God's will is that I be happy? Do I trust that God is a loving God? Do

I have faith in that love, even when circumstances do not reflect it in this moment? This is why the form of prayers you'll be reading are called "affirmative prayers". Affirmative prayer assumes and declares the innate goodness of God and the Universe. It claims that God is right here and right now. In truth, it calls forth the power of the divine. We invite the greatest, most loving Power in the universe, to enter our minds and to heal us. This is the invocation.

Like the Psalms of David, which were often songs of praise, these prayers are meant to open our hearts to God's love and blessings. "The Lord is my shepherd; I shall not want. He maketh me to lie down in green pastures: He leadeth me beside the still waters. He restoreth my soul: he leadeth me on the paths of righteousness for his name's sake." This is the kind of prayer we are learning to master. We trust in God's will and we are not afraid to say specifically how good that will is; for us and for all the world.

Prayer can be like the warm overstuffed comforter we wrap ourselves in on a rainy day or it can be the scrap of wood we cling to adrift in a vast cold ocean as we watch the Titanic sink from view.

Real prayer is a relationship. It is not static. True prayer is an ever evolving, living, breathing relationship between our deepest self and the universal forces. In it's most profound form, it is the relationship with the Divine. At other times it is the relationship with the worldly forces of fear and sacrifice. Nearly every thought we have is some kind of prayer. Like any relationship, it grows from careful attention and cultivation or it withers & dies from lack of care.

There is no communication like the communication that we call prayer. It transcends and uplifts when we open ourselves to its' mystical powers. It is as equally accessible to the king as it is to the slave. God is no respecter of persons and divine love is equally poured out to all who care to make contact with high intention. Yet, we waste the power if we think that prayer is simply a way of getting something. Prayer is most certainly a means to an end, but the end is so much more significant than tangible things. Too many of us go to the Master of all Creation, the limitless Maker of All Things and we settle for crumbs.

To settle for crumbs is to cherish the package instead of the gift that is carefully laid inside. While it may be true that cars, mates, money and "things" can come from prayer, they never really satisfy for long. There is always the need for the next thing. Our thirst is never quenched because we ask for shabby substitutes of the real living waters.

The simple truth is that we live in an abundant universe that was set up to support us all. There are more than enough resources for everyone on the earth to live like millionaires for their entire lives. Yet, we don't all live truly abundant lives because of our obsession with having more. There are those who "have" who do not understand that the greatest abundance comes from sharing what you have. There are those who "have not" who simply resent those who have and continue to think they are victimized by their situation. Both are living under a worldly delusion.

If we could only understand, that at their core, our desires are simply a yearning for God. What we really desire is God...but, God is not some far off stranger. God resides in everyone we meet and we miss the Divine as we pass people by every day. We walk right past the hidden Christ while looking for a new pair of shoes that might be a temporary mood-elevator. We ignore the suffering while we pray for a nicer apartment.

Now, there is nothing wrong with having a nicer apartment. Certainly every one of us has the right to have our basic needs of food, shelter and medical care met. And not just to scrape by either, but to really flourish in this life. Of course if a man is hungry and jobless, then we should most certainly tell him to pray that his physical needs be met by divine action. And, we should join with him in prayer. Then, after we pray, we should allow God to use us personally to take whatever action we can, or that seems most right and helpful to that man, at that moment. For this much is certain; prayer works, but it works most often through people. It is a divine and mystical action but it comes quite beautifully through the human vessel. Therefore, the prayer "God use me," is one of the most effective requests we can make.

Still, I do not wish to encourage anyone to be a "spiritual nitwit" either. There are those who walk the earth thinking they are unattached servants of the Lord who really have just not taken responsibility for their own lives and so other people end up becoming responsible for them. This is not God's will. That is why I say if you need rent money, then don't hesitate to pray for rent money. Even Jesus prayed for his daily bread. Mother Theresa was a woman of prayer, but also a woman of action. I encourage people to do their prayer work being specific about their needs if in a very needful state of mind, but do it with an eye toward the day when these temporary situations will be healed and know that the real prayer then is "Lord, I am yours. Lead me in Your gentle ways and make my life a living testament to the goodness and grace of God. Take my hands and feet and voice and let them serve You."

We should approach prayer as naturally as an intimate conversation with a dear friend; with love, respect and honesty. As with any relationship, it grows and changes over time and blossoms with careful attention. In loving relationships, there is honest sharing, followed by quiet listening. We must not pray "at God." At the end of each prayer, spend time opening up to feel the gentle response which comes.

My purpose in writing this little volume is to give you a spiritual companion on your journey through the rigors and challenges of daily life. Each prayer has been carefully crafted to gently lift you up in consciousness to the place of Divine Aid. I hope you will keep it nearby; in your car, purse, backpack, briefcase or by the bed. My prayer is that you will develop a relationship with these prayers that will expand and enliven your own prayers. The more that you use it, the more deeply the words will sink into your memory and your subconscious mind. Eventually it will become a habit to think the highest, most holy thoughts, all day long.

As for the prayers you will find in this book, there are 4 basic elements that I try to include in most of my affirmative prayers. See if you can recognize them as you read through the book. You may want to include them in the prayers that you may write for yourself.

One element is admitting just what I feel right now. I think it is important at times to acknowledge just what the problem is so that we are not suppressing our deepest feelings. This in itself is helpful in creating some immediate peace.

After admitting what I feel, I move onto the next two elements which are affirmation and denial. I deny that the problem or thought or situation has ultimate power over me. I deny the power of darkness and fear. I reject the idea that anything is more powerful than God in me.

In the affirmative section, I affirm that God is greater than any problem. I claim the power of the Divine to heal me, the situation, and my perception of all things. I state the highest thoughts possible for everything and everyone concerned.

Then, I move into gratitude and praise. I give thanks before anything has even occurred as a statement of my faith that it is already accomplished in the realm of spirit and now it is simply a matter of watching as it manifest into the physical realms.

If you would like more information about this kind of prayer, I suggest you read some of the books by Ernest Holmes who was a master of the affirmative prayer. You may also want to find a local Church of Religious Science or a Unity Church that will support you in learning more about this kind of prayer.

FAILURE AND MAKING MISTAKES
ARE PART OF THE PROCESS OF
SUCCESSFUL LIVING-MAKE YOUR
APOLOGIES, FORGIVE YOURSELF
AND MOVE ON.

# Chapter Two

## *Where Is Your Faith?*

*"Daughter, thy faith hath made the whole; go in peace..."*

Mark 5:34

I could feel that beginning tickle of a scratchy throat. I had a lecture to give in two hours and I wasn't looking forward to speaking for an hour when I was already starting to feel myself falter. My friend Diane sat across from me at the kitchen table and I told her that I hoped I was not catching my god-son's cold. Without even taking a beat she looked up and said, "Where is your faith?"

It was very simply said with no judgment and I knew she wasn't expecting an answer. It wasn't really a question, so much as a reminder. Where was my faith? Did I have faith in the existence and danger of germs that I needed to defend myself against? At that moment, yes, that is where my faith was placed. But, her simple words put things back in proper order. I had the choice of where to place my faith; faith in the Divine or faith in what the physical world throws at me. My return to faith in God was not that I would not get sick, but rather the realization that what I needed to be saved from was the thought that that would be a bad thing.

People will sometimes tell you in times of trouble, "You're never given more than you can handle." This is not my experience nor is it the experience of millions of other people who suffer and die every day. It seems to me that the deeper truth is that I am never given more than *God* can handle.

So this "where is your faith," is a good question. In fact, it is one of the best questions you can ask yourself. I have asked it of myself thousands of times since that day and always it returns me to awareness of the divine.

The question is good because it implies a truth which is this; your faith is always somewhere. You are never without faith. However, it is sometimes "mis-placed"—placed where it does not belong.

Faith itself is a constant attribute of consciousness, where it resides is what is changing and fluctuating. Sometimes our faith is in God, the divine, the goodness of life, and sometimes it is in our money, our intelligence, our wealth or our talents. Perhaps we put our faith in the government or in the law to protect and care for us. Generally speaking, even the most religious among us are unaware of our tendency to have faith in our own abilities. Usually we are running the show—and often with little real success.

The world we see all around us encourages us to put our faith in fear although it names this fear "knowledge." Every day the newspapers and television keep us acutely aware of the danger that lurks everywhere, even in our own homes. In many ways, we bow down to and worship the gods of fear and defense. Over and over we are taught by the voices of fear how to defend ourselves against whatever enemy confronts us. Our lives have become warzones.

At the end of the millennium, we were bombarded by doomsday talk of Armageddon—the last days. The mind is fascinated by the idea of an enemy that is out to get us. What we haven't realized is that we created these enemies through our own fearful thoughts and just as that realm gave birth to the enemy, it can just as surely give rise to thoughts of a savior.

What does this savior save us from? In many ways we are saved from our own cleverness, which has too often been used against us. Experience is teaching us that our fighting gets us nowhere. It's obvious that the war on drugs, the war on poverty, the war on germs and crime have all made the opponents stronger and more clever. Even germs and diseases are getting stronger because of antibiotics.

Everything we fight becomes stronger because it feeds on our attention. That is why we are told in scripture to "resist not evil"—our very resistance gives evil strength. Whatever is the object of our attention receives energy. Therefore, the answer has to be a way of starving the enemy of attention and turning instead toward the light. The answer is a new way of thinking which then gives rise to another way of being and doing—it dawns first in the mind and then radiates outward.

This doesn't mean we pretend that there are no problems or that we ignore the suffering of others. Not at all, in fact, the more time we spend in relationship with divine thinking, the more we grow in compassion and understanding. Ultimately, our faith in divine love increases each time we offer ourselves as servants of that love here on earth. Our own faith, our own convictions are strengthened by giving away what has been given to us. Therefore, we are not just turning away from darkness. We are actually turning toward the Light, and actively using our hands, our feet, and our voices to increase the forces of goodness and beneficence. When enough of us join the ranks of the Lightbearers, the world is literally overtaken by that Light, and the darkness is cast out.

What this means is that there is less time fighting the war against poverty and more time spent creating a society of abundance for everyone. There is less time spent fighting new germs and illnesses, and more time spent awakening the body's own healing immune system. There is more time spent increasing human dignity and self-worth, and less time fighting drugs. This is what the life of prayer and faith can bring.

Now it is our task to awaken. We must acknowledge how much of our time is spent in a constant prayer of fear and dread, and how much time is spent in a prayer to a Higher Power which can deliver us from all fear and pain through the transforming of our minds. There have been times when I have written "where is your faith?" on post-its and put them up on my door to see as I leave the house. Sometimes I put them on my dashboard in my car to remember as I am driving in Los Angeles traffic, or on my computer screen to keep as my mantra all through the day.

Ultimately our faith is always justified one way or another. It's important that we recognize that Jesus often told those he healed that it was their faith that made them whole. Jesus healed the willing. People came to him for this reason and believed with all their hearts that he could perform a miracle. Jesus never tried to convince anyone who did not want the gift. He merely made it available to those who had the faith to receive it. We have total free will as to what we will place our faith and belief in, although many voices in the world are constantly trying to sway our faith their way.

Where is your faith right now? Where have you placed it? Is that the world you want to live in today? Choose you this day what faith you will serve today, for it will most surely come back to serve you.

GOD LOVES YOU
JUST AS YOU ARE,
WITHOUT LIMITS
OR CONDITIONS.

# Chapter Three

## Prayer In Action

*"Trust in the Lord with all thine heart; and lean not unto thine own understanding. In all thy ways acknowledge him, and he shall direct thy paths."*

Proverbs 3:5-6

Prayer is not a passive power, nor are people who pray, lazy people. Sincere prayer is an active force that causes real change first and foremost in the mind of the one who prays. Through this change of mind new actions emerge and they *must* emerge. We think differently and we then act differently in the world. Many of the most dynamic social movements in the world have been led by people who of deep spiritual faith and sincere prayer. These people first turned within for guidance and strength, and then answered the call to take whatever action their internal guidance gave them.

Joan of Arc was no wimp. She heard the voice of God and answered the call. Dr. Martin Luther King, Jr. was a man of deep prayer and yet he led a radical social movement through his peaceful actions. Divine Destiny comes calling for us all, but it is we who must answer the call. When Moses heard the Voice from the burning bush, he was afraid and did not want to follow his calling. He tried to pass it off onto his brother for a while. Eventually, the call was too great to resist and he stepped into his role.

Even Jesus resisted starting his ministry on earth. At the wedding, his first miracle of turning water into wine did not come from his own readiness. His mother, Mary, had to come calling on him to do something, because the wedding party was out of wine. At first he rebuked her saying, "what has this to do with me? My time has not yet come." In other words, he thought he wasn't ready. Thank God for the blessed wisdom of mothers who know us better than we know ourselves.

Too many of us sit waiting for some great sign that the time is right and that it is okay for us to give our gift, to start our ministry, to shine in some way. We wait for permission from "them" whoever "they" are. Many die waiting. Life marches on while you wait. But, miracles save time. The miracle is simply this: the readiness that is most inspiring and helpful is not your own. Personal readiness is not the issue. The issue here is that God is always ready.

We are simply the vessels through which the power flows. Jesus perhaps was not yet ready in his own mind, but the Father was ready to use him in the now, not at some future date when everything feels more comfortable or safe. Jesus had prepared himself through study and prayer. We all must do our part to be prepared for the opportunities that will most surely come, but the timing is not up to us to determine.

Yes, it is true that there is a lot to be said for timing. But, divine timing is always ready. Of course you should not go rushing in totally unprepared for the situation ahead, but that is what divine guidance is for. We go to the upper-room to ask, to inquire, to seek for the answer. Deep in the center of your being, YOU KNOW. There is a knowing that cannot be denied, that must be listened to and followed if there is to be any internal peace.

When I began writing this book several years ago, I was very excited at the thought that my parents would be so happy about it. Well, both my parents passed away while this book sat gathering dust on publisher's desks. I kept listening more to the voices of the world than my own internal guidance. Yes, I was praying for help and guidance, and I was declaring divine right action, but I did not yet have the conviction and confidence of my own knowing. I thought that the "powers that be" knew more than I did. I spent too much time second-guessing myself. I didn't want to seem pushy or arrogant. I was waiting for permission because I thought others knew better than what my gut was telling me.

Basically, all the publishers said the same kind of thing, "there are too many prayer books already." When I gave the very first teeny tiny little draft idea of this to Marianne Williamson, she was instrumental in getting me to write more and more prayers; she said, "Jacob, there can never be too many prayers written." I knew that she was right and I listened to her wise counsel and have held onto it through all the rejections. You know, nobody says, "oh, there are too many mystery books already, too many romance novels, too many cookbooks, too many horror novels." It is assumed there is an unquenchable thirst for these topics, particularly if there is drama, gossip or fear involved. Bring up the subject of God, and people can get very uncomfortable, very quickly.

One of the first agents who looked at it wrote, "I am uncomfortable with the feel-good Christian content." Really, how dare I help people feel good? It all seems so silly now. Obviously, if you read a few of the prayers, you can see that they are non-dogmatic and of no specific religion or faith. My purpose here is to be accepting and inclusive of all faiths and all beliefs, as best I can, without interrupting the flow by trying too hard to be politically correct. My own personal feeling is that God encompasses both male and female. I may use the names God, Him, Her, Divine Mother, Angel, Christ or Lord, because that is my own personal vocabulary, but you can change the names or genders to whatever opens your heart the most. The spirit of God is not limited by names.

It seems that the only way to make sure that we don't upset anyone is to say nothing at all or to make what we so say generic that no one even knows what we're talking about. How can there be true creativity in this environment? How can miracles happen when everyone is so afraid to make a mistake or say the wrong thing? How can we really give our unique expression of creative divinity on earth if we are consumed by whether or not it will sell to the masses? Having a "hook" to sell a product certainly doesn't seem like a term of love and contribution to me. As long as our intention is to love, and we ask for God's help, we will be guided, but we must let go of the need for the approval of the world.

The other day I ran into an old friend. We talked about his life a bit and then he said to me, "don't you ever wish you had more luck?" I tactfully pointed out that I thought he was spoiled and ungrateful. I said that he and I have more than the majority of people on the planet simply because we live in the United States and have jobs. But at the same time, we are bred as Americans to be such go-getters that we often don't take time to appreciate the good that is already here and now. We are always comparing ourselves to others who just seem to have more or be more. His major concern was not about the content of his life, but rather about the form it was taking. I suspect he'd forgotten the importance of gratitude and contribution. His thoughts were all about what he was not getting, rather than what he already had and what he could contribute to others.

What I said I'd like more of is not luck, but courage. With courage to do what we came to earth to do, life just flows forward and things work. The courage to answer the inner-call and listen to our own guidance guarantees a life of meaning and substance. When we have the courage and discipline to turn away from thinking of what we are going to get out of a situation, what it will do for us, how it will take care of us or guarantee our future and instead focus on the sheer joy of giving and creating…this frees up so much energy and aliveness that the future takes care of itself because it is merely an extension of the present.

Something wonderful happens to the psyche of one whose life is one of contribution. To give of yourself and your life's energy is a great act of faith. This is not a life of sacrifice and deprivation. This is not about giving until you have nothing left to give. You must open up to receive if you are ever going to truly contribute. However, we cannot wait until we have before we give. There is always something we can contribute and this is what it means to put our prayers into action. This means we are not waiting for God to show up, we are busy showing up for God even if no one seems to care yet. If you keep showing up long enough, eventually you will rise to the top because everyone else quits when they don't get what they want.

I suggest you look at your own life now. Is there something that you've been passively waiting for? Have you placed the power in the hands of some external person or situation? Are you waiting for luck or destiny to come and find you before you show up at 100%? Ask the Holy Spirit if it's time to take action. Life marches by so quickly. There is someone somewhere waiting for you to arrive.

## Chapter Four

# The Divine Experiment

*"Prove me now herewith, saith the Lord of hosts, if I will not open the windows of heaven, and pour you out a blessing, that there will not be room to receive it."*

Malachi 3:10

Now comes the next step in your journey. It is now time to go beyond mere theory and put these ideas into actual daily practice. In order to stop tormenting yourself with your thoughts, it is necessary to replace those old fearful thoughts with new divine thoughts. In order to do that I ask you to try the "divine experiment." You have nothing to lose but your misery.

I am asking you to begin a 90 day plan of mental/spiritual cleansing and renewal. All that is required is a bit of time each day, preferably in the morning as soon after waking as possible. Before you start this daily practice, go through the prayers which follow, finding the ones that apply to your life right now and keeping in mind the others which are there when you need them. Then, go through and do the exercises section. It is very important to fill out the personal prayer and your mission statement.

Please do change the prayers to fit your own spiritual understanding. I have used the words and style that is most appropriate for me, but it is only my personal preference. I believe that God is both male and female. Therefore, I have used both Father and Mother throughout the book, but you may change that to whatever is most meaningful to you. The daily affirmative prayer uses the name Jesus at one point, but you may want to use the word Angel, or Christ, or Higher Power-whatever works for you personally is what is best.

Prayer is not a magic pill or a quick fix. These prayers are designed to add to your tool kit of mind, body and spirit healing. The prayers and exercises are here to help you. Use the ones that help and forget the ones that don't. They are not written to take the place of physical exercise, medication or psychotherapy. I don't expect that you will read a prayer and necessarily have an instant healing. However, at the same time, it is important to remember that God is bigger than whatever problem or issue you are experiencing today. Miracles do happen, but they are not under our control. All the wisdom, all the answers, all the help you could ever need is within you. That help has been placed there by God as you own inner-light, but you must seek within through consistent daily prayer and meditation. You must listen for the answers.

Someone once said to me, "I tested the prayer for depression with a friend who is clinically depressed and he thought it was no help at all." I'm not surprised. Yes, instant healing can occur, however usually the effects of prayer are cumulative. I'm sure he didn't take one anti-depressant and say, "This stuff is no help at all" after only one day. How silly to work out at the gym for the first time and that afternoon say, "Exercise doesn't work. I am still flabby and weak." Another man told me that he'd been on prozac for ten years and recently changed to another anti-depressant because the prozac didn't help him. I doubt that many people would say a prayer every day for more than a week if they felt it wasn't helping right away much less give it ten years of effort. This brings us back again to how much more faith many people have in the things of the world rather than the things of God.

I believe that prayer brings immediate comfort, but to really change our lives, we must make a serious commitment to daily prayer even when things are going great. Mind, body and spirit must each have daily deposits made into their accounts. I think that if someone is taking anti-depressants that it would be helpful to bless the pill as you take it and then say the prayer for comforting depression. I am not minimizing the agony of depression. But, I am maximizing the ecstasy of God. You see, I have been depressed, really depressed. I know what it's like to sob for an hour in the shower every day, to not get dressed for weeks, to lose weight to the point of near anorexia, to not want to live another day. It took work on my body, mind and spirit to exit the tunnel, but prayer and faith was, for me, the greatest part of the light at the end of that tunnel.

I have been in therapy with wonderful results. I make time for regular exercise and I take medicine when I am ill. I simply bless whatever I am doing as an instrument of the Divine. Medicine, exercise, vitamins and psychotherapy are not at odds with the spiritual life. Therapists, nurses, doctors, massage therapists, counselors, surgeons, acupuncturists, social workers, personal coaches, chiropractors and many other kinds of healers can be part of God's plan for personal restoration. God can work through whatever channels are used if we include Him. In fact, prayer can be the avenue that leads you to the right doctors and medicines.

So, here is the invitation to the Divine Experiment. The experiment to see if affirmative prayer really can have a positive effect on your life. **Each day for the next 90 days**, begin by reading the daily affirmative prayer, your own personal prayer, prayers for others, and your mission statement. If there is a prayer which meets the situation that you are presently facing, read that one every day as well. Read the prayers slowly. If you can do it out loud, that is best. If not, simply drink in the meaning as you silently read and think about what the prayer says. Fill your mind with each image. In addition, I strongly suggest that young people read the daily prayer creed for teenagers and young people. All of this takes very little time. If you have extra time, you may want to write in a journal afterwards. In fact, it is great idea to keep a journal in which you can record your process and even make a list of things that begin to change and manifest in your life and in your awareness.

The prayers will create change only through the use of them. If they are used sporadically, they will have a sporadic effect. But, if you think of this book as your own little portable spiritual/mental tool kit, it will serve you through many daily situations. Keep it close for quick reference. I keep one in my backpack for any time when I am feeling myself get tense and upset. I can then quickly refer to whatever prayer or exercise is most appropriate.

The exercises for the healing process have helped me in many situations in which I was about to lose my temper. The affirmations page has often kept me centered while waiting in line somewhere. The prayer for dealing with rejection has helped when I was sending this manuscript out to publishers. The completion prayer has been very helpful in situations in which I am beating myself up with regrets about some situation in which I feel I blew it. In the past 4 years these prayers have helped me through the deaths of both my parents, my foster-sister and through many other challenges.

You may want to have a prayer partner or join a prayer group during this process. I have been in a prayer group for the past 3 years and had a few prayer partners during that time. A prayer partner is simply someone who agrees supports you in your prayer requests and joins with you in prayer. You and your prayer partner include one another in your daily prayers. You are not there to counsel one another or give advice. Just listen and support.

There is a mystical power that enters these relationships and makes the power of the prayers awesome. You may meet informally once a week to simply briefly discuss your present situations, say who and what you are praying for and about, and then pray together. You may choose to read some of the prayers from this book together at times, but then be sure to say your own prayers as well. Simply speak from your heart. God hears and understands.

Try the experiment for 90 days. Notice how your thoughts begin to change bit by bit and how that changes your days and nights. You are worth the effort. You are worth the commitment to yourself. Love yourself enough to nurture yourself this way. God needs you. The world needs you. We need you. We are waiting for you to shine even more brightly than you already do.

TO FORGIVE SOMEONE DOES NOT EXCUSE THEIR BAD BEHAVIOR NOR DOES IT MEAN "THEY WON;" IT MEANS THAT YOU HAVE STOPPED PLAYING THE BLAME GAME AND WANT TO BE FREE.

# *Chapter Five*

## *The Prayers*

*"Prayer is not an old woman's idle amusement. Properly understood and applied, it is the most potent instrument of action."*

Mahatma Gandhi

# Daily Affirmative Prayer

God is with me now. He has a plan for my life.
I believe in the power of God. I believe in miracles.
I believe in the radical action of God's love here on Earth.
There is no opposite to this power—it flows from God through
me now.
All love and compassion fills my heart.
God uses my hands, my feet and my voice this day to do His will.
All good is effortlessly drawn to me today.
I cannot fail to be at the right place at the right time.
There is limitless good—more than enough for everyone.
All fear and negativity are washed clean from me now.
There is no need to worry or rush, the Universe has perfect timing.
I embrace this new day and the miracles it brings.
I am a radiant beam of light that attracts friends,
love, success, good health and joy.
I am not afraid to be happy today. I am not afraid of love.
Love and acknowledgment shine on me from all directions today.
People are drawn to me and love to assist me in truly helpful ways
My business and all my affairs are run by Divine Intelligence.
I always have more than enough money to pay all my bills
and to live an abundant lifestyle.
This is a rich season of Divine Harvest.
My body radiates good health and energy as this is the
pure reflection of God's love.
I am never alone nor lonely for my brother Jesus is here beside me.

I breathe life in deeply and I am relaxed and at peace.
My mind is clear and my heart is full of love for all of life.
Nothing wavers me from my truth today. All that I need is given me.
I have no lack of any good thing.
There is a power in me. I have my Father's power to heal and reveal.
My relationships are loving and intimate.
My appetites are made right by the principle of perfect assimilation.
Every organ and cell of my body is alive with Divine Intelligence.
This intelligence keeps the flow of energy and health at an
optimum.
I maintain my perfect weight and desire the best foods and
exercise.
All mental, physical and emotional habits which are not of
a sweet and loving nature now drop from my atmosphere.
I deserve love and companionship and I am open
to receive that love now in the form of my right mate.
The Universe has chosen the right one and
that person is welcomed by me now.
I accept an intimate relationship and I am happy.
My family and loved ones are surrounded by
the white light of Divine Protection.
I am thankful to the Father for all this good and for my life.
I step back now and allow the Universe to do the work.
I do not interfere nor doubt.
I trust that it is done and so it is.
Amen

# A Prayer For The Children Of The World

The Divine Father Mother Presence is now
blessing all the children of the world.
Each one is now held safely in the arms of
an angel of God who guides and protects
them all through the day and night.
All parents everywhere are now being filled
with loving-kindness, patience and wisdom.
All the resources necessary to raise a healthy,
happy and successful child are now being drawn into their lives.
There are more than enough resources in the
Universe to care for all the children of the world
and even now the leaders and citizens of
every country and nation are being Divinely
guided and supported to care for the health,
educational, spiritual, financial
and emotional needs of the world's youth.
Every school, park, playground and home is protected and held
perfectly in the hands of God.
Here and now, I give God my hands, my feet and
my voice, that I may be used to make the world a safer and more
wonderful place for all children to grow and thrive in.
I allow myself to be used in the service of
helping to raise up a society of
healthy and happy adults.

I send out my loving thoughts now as a beacon of light which shines outward into every street of the world, blanketing the globe with God's love and safety.

We are all healed together.

The family, whatever form it takes,

is restored by Divine Love this very day.

I thank You Lord for hearing my prayer

and for the manifestations of good which now

follow—I release this prayer to You now in

full faith knowing that it is done by Your

Holy Spirit for the highest good of all concerned.

And so it is.

Amen

# Prayer For My Daughter

Dear Divine Mother, bless this child of mine.
I know that this precious girl was sent from the Light
and is held by the Angels.
I am merely a vessel through which God's love flows.
I let go of my own goals and agendas for my child
so that she might find her own great destiny.
Even now everything that is good, beautiful and holy is being
irresistibly drawn to her.
May she have everything needed to live a life of joy, success and
great happiness.
Love is her natural state of being and I know that God is
the Source of all her needs. I release her to You now.
May I be here when she needs me but not squelch her by
following too closely.
Help me to balance freedom and responsibility.
May she grow into the fullness of her femininity.
May she cultivate the friendships of other women.
May she find her own center of power within and
not seek in the world for her approval.
Let her never shrink from her own intelligence.
May she find her place in the world.
May she love greatly and be loved in return.
May she love and accept her body as it is and as it is not.
May she grow in physical strength and health.

May her mind and eyes be open that she may grow in wisdom and compassion.
May the world be blessed for her having been here.
Thank You for sending her here to be with us.
Amen

## Prayer For My Son

Heavenly Father, embrace my Son in Your Love.
I place him in Your hands now that he may walk in Light.
Strengthen his heart and mind and keep him safe from harm.
May he grow into the man You would have him be.
May he be a man of honor, compassion and truth.
Keep him strong in faith that he may be guided
only by Your Voice within him.
Strengthen his body but, may his strength never be used in anger.
May compassion temper his judgment.
Open his mind that he may have empathy and patience
with those whose views are different from his own.
Let him never carry his burdens alone nor
think it weak to ask for help.
Source him and be his supply that he may prosper & succeed.
Help him to keep the adventurous heart of a boy
but with the maturity of a man.
May he have a tender heart and a keen mind.
May his work be a joy to him.
May he laugh every day but never at the expense of another.
May he understand the importance of family.
May he honor women and his fellow man.
Help me Lord, to hold the light for him
without my shadow interfering with his path.
I entrust him into Your care.

Thank You for this gift.
May he bless the world.
Amen

## Affirmative Prayer For Children

God placed in me a beautiful light,
That guides and protects me all day and all night.
I am His child and am filled
with His love,
And angels surround me
below and above.
I know I'm exactly who
I'm supposed to be,
Everyone loves me
for just being me.
Thank You God for
watching over our family.
Amen

IT IS <u>NEVER</u> TOO LATE FOR A MIRACLE. GOD IS ALWAYS RIGHT ON TIME.

# Daily Prayer Creed for Young People & Teenagers

I am as God created me and I am exactly what I was meant to be.
There is a beautiful spirit within me that holds and protects me
all through the day and night.
Nothing and no one can diminish this perfect Spirit inside me.
There are no words nor actions from outside of me that can
change this beautiful beam of light which I am.
I came to Earth to be just who and what I am and
I have a wonderful job to do.
All that I need in order to do what I came here to do is provided
for me by Divine Substance and Supply.
I am surrounded by unseen angels who love me and watch over me.
I am a unique person in the Universe and no one can take my place
or fill the role I came here to play.
My heart is filled with love overflowing for myself and for
those closest to me. I am a special person and I recognize my
brilliance.
I came to love the world and I have my own way of making that
love manifest.
I am willing to rise above all circumstances in order to accept
my part
in healing the world by living with integrity, love,
honor, compassion and goodness.
Today I will not judge myself nor anyone I meet.
Today I will treat myself as a precious human treasure.
Today I will know that I matter.

Today I will tell someone else that they matter too.
Oh Lord, thank You for making me just the way I am.
I will not criticize Your work today by judging myself.
Instead, I humbly ask that You make any changes in me that You
see fit and I will love, honor and cherish whatever remains.
From this day on I will not harm myself in any way.
I will treat myself as a vessel of the living spirit of Love.
I will not be tempted by anyone or anything to abuse or dishonor
myself.
I surrender my relationship with my parents and my family to You.
May we grow in love, communication and understanding.
May all our needs be provided for this very day.
Lord, help me to live in love today.
Protect me and those I love.
Please bless my family.
Shine Your light on us now.
Pour Your blessings on us.
I give my life to You.
Thank You God that this is so.
Amen

# Prayer For Our Parents

The Christ in me calls forth the Christ in my parents.
We are One in God.
I honor them now for giving birth to me.
I am grateful to God for whatever good they have given me.
I claim that I am heir to what they did right and I let go of their mistakes.
I am filled with compassion.
I release my father and mother into God's care.
They are blessed and embraced by Divine Love.
All their needs are taken care of this very day.
Their bodies and health are sustained by God.
They are filled with vital energy.
Their finances come from Divine Supply.
There are limitless resources for their abundant life, prosperity and happiness.
Joy fills their hearts and their minds are clear and calm.
They are safe from harm and free from fear.
Their good cannot be denied for it comes from God Himself.
I forgive and release my parents from the past.
I release myself from the past.
We are encircled by the light of deep forgiveness and acceptance.
We are set free from the bondage of our past roles and are free to be who we truly are at depth.
I let go of trying to make sense of the past.
May we now step into a dynamic present.

I let go of the form and accept Divine Content.
I am grateful to God for the freedom of this healing.
And so it is.
And so I let it be.
Amen

## Bedtime Prayer

The Divine Father Mother Presence of God
now enters my consciousness as I let go of the day.
I let go of all that went wrong and all that went right.
I now recognize my mistakes and release them into
His forgiveness. I accept with grace the lessons learned.
I let go of those who may have hurt or offended me.
I will not take my anger to bed and so I forgive as best I can.
As I sleep, all my worries dissolve and I rest in God.
I give thanks for this day.
While I sleep, my family and loved ones are
all held safely in the arms of God.
My sleep is restful and healing.
My body and mind relax and let go.
My dreams are peaceful and teach me
what God would have me know.
I invite the Angels to now enter my mind that they may
guide me to the Higher Realms of Consciousness.
My home and all who abide here are filled with
Divine love which protects us from all harm.
All are safe in His care this night.
As I turn my eyes from the outer world I am
filled with the assurance that God is in control.
May my sleep give me the rest I need that
tomorrow I may do better.
May I be made into the person that

God would have me be.
For this I am so grateful
So it is.
Amen

# Preparation Prayer

I relinquish all fear and control to Father Mother God.
My Holy Guide has brought me this far and will not abandon me now.
I am not alone. I have Divine Assistance.
There is no need for fear or worry for God is here beside me.
I let go of trying to control circumstances and surrender into His will.
All the brightest and the best within me is brought forward this day.
The Light of God shines brightly in me and radiates out into all I do and say.
My thoughts are high, my spirit soars, and my heart is open wide.
I breathe deeply and release all nervousness and fear.
All anxiety dissolves into Divine Confidence.
I give this situation to the Source of all good to control.
All outcomes are placed in the hands of the perfect love of God.
All people, places and situations are now brought in line
with Spiritual truth. There are no obstructions to God's plan.
Nothing can delay or impede the will of God.
My body and mind are peaceful, calm and relaxed.
There is nothing to fear.
There is nothing to get—no need to make anything happen.
I let go of all resistance. I let go of all pain.
Thank You God for walking with me now.
Thank You for caring.

Thank You for the Divine Solution to all problems.
Thank You for Divine Strength to accept all things.
I release this to You now knowing that all unfolds
perfectly according to Your will for the
highest good of all concerned.
So it is.
Amen

# Completion Prayer

God can heal all things.
I now surrender this experience to God.
I acknowledge myself for showing up and doing my best.
Whatever mistakes I may have made are
healed by Divine Restoration.
I forgive myself now so that God may enter my mind.
My heart is filled with forgiveness for any mistakes
that were made by another.
Christ-in-me is more powerful than any particular situation.
I am at the effect of God alone.
There is nothing to control, obsess or worry about.
God is in charge and all is well.
Divine process is at work here and there is a plan for the greater good.
My good is never withheld from me.
I am always at choice in my perceptions and thoughts.
I choose to see things with miraculous perception.
The peace of God washes away all fear and anxiety.
I call on and claim Divine Right Action for all aspects of this situation.
God's plan is one in which everyone wins.
I accept His plan now.
I let go of this experience now and surrender every aspect of it to God.

If there is something still to be done I will be told by Divine
Wisdom.
All is well in the hands of God.
I slow down my thoughts.
I breathe deeply.
I relax.
I let go.
Thank You God.
Amen

# Prayer For The World

God is with us now. He has a plan for the world.
I believe that God is all good and everywhere present.
I believe in the power of His love here on Earth.
I believe that He wills that the planet be healed.
I now begin to see the world as God would have it be.
All life is now cradled in His loving arms.
There is no place on Earth that His light does not touch.
I now call upon His holy name to heal this world.
Divine Love is now flowing through every country and nation.
Every man, woman and child is embraced in perfect love.
There is no poverty, pain, sickness nor lack in God.
This is an abundant universe and there are more than
enough resources for everyone to have all that they need.
Every person and nation now draws to them all that they need
in order to be happy, healthy, safe and loved.
Under God's plan everyone wins and no one loses.
Greed, addictions, anger, prejudice and sickness
all dissolve in the miracle of Divine Restoration.
The need to be right is released and dissolves.
All of nature is being brought into harmony as
the plants, animals and all living things
are restored to their natural state of being.
The citizens and leaders of every nation are now
being awakened to the truth of our Oneness.
All beings everywhere are being lifted up to their highest and best.

We recognize the sacredness of all life.
We are all healed together.
Here and now I give my life to God that I may be used as
an instrument of healing and change.
I recognize my importance in this plan for salvation of the
world.
May I do no harm. May I help wherever I can.
Use me, Lord. I am Yours.
Amen

# Centering Prayer

I now turn inward to the Center of my Being where God abides.
I go the well of Infinite Goodness and Wisdom.
There is a perfect Presence within me that now radiates love
throughout my entire being—I am at home here.
I invoke and awaken the Christ Consciousness within me.
I dip into the Divine Center of Infinite Supply.
Calmness, peace and tranquillity are mine.
The Father and I are One.
Nothing can pull or distract me from the truth of my spirit-self.
I come inside where I am sheltered by God's love and warmth.
The Divine Presence within me now speaks to me of who and
what I am.
All through the day and night I am reminded of the power that
is in all beings everywhere.
I choose from this moment on to see God in all things.
I now remember who I am and where I came from.
Nothing and no one can separate me from the love of God.
I am not alone for He is here beside me.
Every breath that I take heals my worried mind.
There is nothing to control. Nothing to change.
I accept the perfection of this moment just as it is.
I know that I am one with God and His voice
within me speaks to me clearly now.
I thank You Divine Father for hearing me and for the
manifestations of good which now follow.

I now release everything to the all-loving inner presence.
I surrender myself and all that I am to the Mother-Father God .
All is well. I am loved.
Thank You God.
So be it.
Amen

## Relationship Prayer For Singles

There is a bright beam of light shining
from the heart of God directly into mine.
Divine Love opens my heart like a flower in the sunlight.
I am filled with love overflowing and I allow myself to love all
people.
I am not afraid of intimate love.
My consciousness now expands to make room for my right mate
to enter.
I include this person in my world and
I deeply surrender all fears and barriers.
God now creates a relationship that is healthy, fun, loving,
supportive and based on deep abiding friendship.
I know that I deserve love and that with God all things are possible.
There is no lack in God and none in me.
There is more than enough love for everyone.
I am not held back by any circumstances for God is all powerful.
My age, my past, my mistakes, my frailties, my quirks and
character defects cannot obstruct nor delay the power of the Holy
Spirit.
I am whole and complete just as I am. Nothing can keep my
good away.
I no longer attract shadow figures from my past for I am healed
and forgiven.
I release with love all my past relationships and accept their
important

part in my learning and growth. Here and now I am reborn.
All is made right in this holy instant.
There is no need to seek for a relationship nor for a person.
My right relationship already exists in the mind of God.
My awareness now expands so that I may recognize
the answer to my prayer when it arrives.
The Holy Spirit has chosen the right person and
I accept that person into my life now.
We are being drawn together by Divine Right Action.
I do not strain nor worry for I know that our relationship,
it's timing, and all it's circumstances rest in God's hands.
I give thanks now as I release this to Him in full-faith knowing
that all will happen according to His will
for the highest good of all concerned.
And so it is.
Praise God.
Amen

## Relationship Prayer For Couples

God has brought us together and
our relationship has been touched by Him.
I place this relationship in His care.
I believe that love is the greatest truth.
This love is a source of joy and inspiration to us both.
My heart is filled with gratitude for this gift.
I claim our blessings now and know that all that we need comes
to us.
Divine Supply sustains us.
Angels surround us and support our lives.
We are safe to love and be loved.
We are free to laugh and play together.
It is safe for us to relax into this happiness.
I commit myself this day to the highest love of which I am capable.
We are safe to share the truth without attack.
We truly know and see each other.
We are a safe space for one another. Our love blesses and supports us.
We have been drawn together by God's power for His purposes.
God sustains and sources every aspect of our love.
Words of praise and acknowledgment flow freely and abundantly.
Intimacy, tenderness and good humor fill our conversations.
All past guilt and negative patterns are released and we are set free.
Jealousy, envy and mistrust are washed away and find no home
in us.
All power struggles dissolve and we relax into the Divine Flow.

Trust and honesty grow daily in our hearts and minds.
We choose to focus on love and to let go of the rest.
God chooses the form which is perfect for our ultimate happiness.
Judgments and criticism cease as we acknowledge the best in one another.
Our physical relationship is loving, stimulating and fulfilling.
All communications are filtered through the Divine Veil
and only what is loving and true is heard.
God Himself corrects every mistake.
Patience and compassion rule our hearts.
We receive all that we give.
Thank You Lord for this precious gift.
Thank You for the blessing of this magnificent person.
Thank You for our love.
Thank You for our lives.
We are blessed.
So it is.
Amen

*Struggle is often a sign that you are trying to control life again. How blissful to simply surrender to God.*

# Prayer For Career/Work

God has called me by my name and I am His.
He has a place for me in this world and it is the place I want to
be.
There is no place nor position in which I cannot work for Him.
I now allow myself to be lifted to what He would have me do.
In all things I seek and find the glory of serving God
by serving the people who are sent to me.
This day, right now I am in my right place for this particular day.
I am happy and humbled that I may be of use for
however long this work serves His purposes.
I recognize that God's will is that I be happy, loved and successful.
I surrender into His will now.
That which I love to do brings me great joy, prosperity,
Satisfaction, and a sense of accomplishment.
God brings to me all that is mine.
I deserve a work environment in which there is mutual support
in calling forth our best talents, creativity and inner-resources.
I know that this is God's will.
All the assistance and resources to do this job with excellence
now come to me quickly and easily.
There is no strain and my atmosphere supports me in
bringing forth my highest and best.
God is the source of my supply and so I
am always well compensated for my work.
My right work thrives and flourishes.

My work is unaffected by current economic changes and trends.
My stability rests on Divine Economics.
There is an ever-expanding and limitless inflow of good.
Love permeates my thoughts, words and actions and
this is an attractive energy.
My work is appreciated and acknowledged.
I let go of all past work experiences and beliefs about my career.
I let go of what other people think for I care only what God thinks.
I know that I have Divine Approval.
I allow myself to receive my good.
I am so happy to be given this opportunity to serve in joy.
Thank You God. Thank You God. Thank You God.
Amen

# Physical Healing

There is a Divine Physician within me.
Eternal wisdom and healing abide in me.
I place my body in the care of the Supreme Intelligence.
This Intelligence is in every living thing that exists and
It exists in me now.
It perfectly runs my body to it's fullest potential.
This Intelligence is the same power that
Jesus used to heal the sick and the dead.
I call on that Power now to make Itself known in me.
Right now Divine Love is coursing through my veins into
my organs and into every cell of my body.
Every breath I take relaxes my muscles, eases all tensions and
makes my mind peaceful and still.
There is nothing to strive for nor against-
no illness to resist nor condition to battle.
Whatever is happening in my body is loved and accepted,
for anything that is not a reflection of perfect love is temporary.
Divine Intelligence knows exactly how to run my body perfectly.
In divine truth my body is healthy and fit and it feels good.
I love and bless my body just as it is and just as it is not.
It is a temporary vehicle and I appreciate every detail the
Creator made.
I allow myself to enjoy healthy foods and exercise.
All that I do contributes to my health and vitality.
I allow myself to be fully alive.

I do not use my body for safety nor to hide.
My body is free of my past emotions and thoughts.
I release any addictions or disorders for they have
no power in the presence of the Holy Spirit.
Only the laws of God apply to my health.
I forgive myself for any harm I may have done to my body
in the past—it is over now and can have no effect.
I identify myself with Spirit and not with the flesh.
I give thanks to my body for all that it has done for me.
I give thanks to God for healing it now.
And so it is.
Amen

# Forgiveness

God is healing me now.
I can no longer weary myself with my judgments.
I call to mind those whom I feel have harmed me
or withheld from me what is mine.
Together we are released from the prison I have made for us.
I let go of who is right and who is wrong.
There is no resentment in God and none in me.
I am free in this holy moment of release as I allow God to heal
my broken heart, my frightened, angry mind and my tired soul.
I call upon His Holy Spirit to come into me and make me whole.
I know that the Spirit within me is safe from all harm and
that everything that is mine now comes to me.
Divine Action is compelling all people, places and circumstances
to result in a happy conclusion for everyone concerned.
I do not question Divine Wisdom in this.
No one and nothing can come between me and my good.
No mistake can harm me for I live and move in God.
No lack of any kind can touch the child of God.
I am that child of God.
The Angel of compassion now surrounds me with her beautiful
light and that light fills my mind and quenches my thirsting soul.
My heart is opening up to see what God would have me see
in all those whom I have judged or been judged by.
Peace fills the empty chambers of my heart as I now let go of
the past.

From this moment on I choose to look away from
the errors of myself and others.
I choose to learn what God would have me learn
from this situation now as I let it go.
I choose this day to seek and find the good,
the beautiful and the holy in all God's children.
This relationship is now released to God and I am happy that it
is so.
Thank You Lord for hearing my prayer.
I trust in Your will.
And so it is.
Amen

# Wedding Day Prayer

Heavenly Creator, we join with you today
as the dearly beloved of this beautiful couple.
We stand here now as the Holy Witnesses to a most sacred and
holy union and we lift them up to Your Light today that
You may pour out your blessings upon them.
This day is dedicated to a great and powerful love created by You.
As they have been drawn together by this love,
may it draw us all closer together here and now.
We stand together now as a spiritual community to
bear witness to the love and promises given and received.
We commit ourselves now to holding a sacred space in our
hearts and minds for this couple to flourish and grow.
We accept this sacred honor and take seriously our task to
hold the light for _____ and _____.
Lord, strengthen their love and renew their lives this day that
they may have serious intentions and light hearts.
May their lives blossom and grow in love, health, abundance
and joy.
May all conflicts and differences be quickly resolved and forgiven.
May angels surround and bless their family and their home.
May all who know them be blessed by the presence of such a
great love.
Thank You Lord for this new family
Thank You for this glorious day.
Amen

## Prayer For The Bride

Divine Mother, I am filled with the light of radiant love today.
Pour out your blessings on me this day as I pledge myself to
a most precious and intimate love.
I open my heart now to receive my beloved.
I make a space for him to live inside of me.
I take his hand this day to walk forward on a mystical and
courageous journey.
I now allow my beauty to shine forth as never before.
I do not shrink back from the glory of who I am on this holy day.
This day unfolds effortlessly and joyfully according to Divine Will.
There is nothing to worry about, nothing to control—all is well.
I relax into the process and let God take care of all the details.
My light flows forth in all directions and I allow myself to fully
receive all the blessings that are here for me today.
I breathe in the rich splendor of all that I see and feel today.
I am held in the arms of Divine Love today and I extend that
love to all who come to witness this sacred event.
I graciously accept the gift of my beloved today.
I surrender myself gladly to our love.
May this love fill our home and our hearts.
May patience, kindness and joy rule our love.
May my womanhood flower to its fullest strength and power in
his love.
May his manhood grow in gentle patience and wisdom in my
presence.

May Divine Love find a home in us now.
Thank you for this day and for this love.
Amen

## Prayer For The Groom

Heavenly Father, I am humbled and grateful
to have found such a great and glorious love in this world.
I stand joyfully before You today ready to receive this beautiful
gift
and ready to surrender myself to it's majesty.
I am filled with grace today.
I breathe in deeply and allow myself to be fully alive.
Each breath opens my heart more and more as it calms my
mind.
I am fully present and I allow the events to unfold before me.
The Spirit of Divine Love rules this day.
As I commit myself to this awesome love I allow
myself to drink in her beauty and to receive her into my heart.
I honor the mystery that she is.
I make room for her in my life and in my heart.
I cherish what she has brought to my life and I shall do my best
to never be stingy with my compliments or in showering her with
my love.
I allow myself to grow into my full manhood by honoring
the Divine Woman who dwells within my beloved.
May we walk together through all things in love and harmony.
May God bless us and our family all the days of our lives.
Thank You Father for this miraculous day.
Amen.

# Prayer To Conceive A Child

Oh Divine Creator, we open ourselves to receive the gift of a precious child.
We make ready now the consciousness of our home and
open our lives to welcome this new life.
Our bodies, hearts and minds are fertile ground
for the planting of this divine seed.
From this moment on we treat ourselves and one another with
love, care and nurturing for we know this is a
sacred and holy task that we undertake together.
We now call forth some tender little spirit to find a home here.
Relaxing into the Divine Flow of life we allow the process
to unfold in its own perfect timing and way.
Lord, if this is the right time, we now open ourselves to receive this.
May all that we do and say be infused with this loving intention.
May we be the parents that You would have us be.
May our lives be a safe haven to guide and protect.
May the love that we have for one another now expand and
multiply in the form of a child.
We surrender this prayer to You.
We trust in the process and in the Divine Wisdom of all that
unfolds.
Our desires are placed in Your hands and in Your heart.
Thank You Lord.
Amen

# Prayer For Safe Pregnancy & Birth

God, I place myself into Your hands.
The preciousness of this life within me fills me with gratitude
and I am humbled by the magnitude of this miracle.
I now allow the Divine Wisdom of this process to take over.
I allow myself to be nurtured, helped and supported.
At this very moment Divine Light is filling my body.
Divine Wisdom knows exactly how to run my body and to
create, nurture and sustain the life that is within me.
Every moment the Divine Mother within me is
giving us all that we need for a happy and healthy pregnancy.
I now release my fears and relax into this natural and
miraculous process.
My body's changes are welcomed and accepted.
It is okay for me to be emotional and to feel things deeply.
I am beautiful and know that I am a part of the precious cycle
of life.
My body knows what it needs and I am irresistibly drawn to
the right
foods, exercises, books, physicians as I listen to my internal
wisdom.
I am being carried by God.
The birth process is witnessed and supported by the angels.
I relax into the process as my baby comes easily and safely into
this world.
May angels surround us all and guide this dear spirit

here to Earth at just the right moment.
I accept this blessing with a humble heart.
Thank You Lord.
Amen

# Prayer For A Sick Child

Dear God, I turn to You now that You may shine
Your healing light on this child.
It is so difficult and painful to see this innocent one
suffering even for a moment.
Banish from this little body all pain, sickness and disease.
Use my hands as instruments of Divine Healing—move through
me now.
Restore, strengthen and renew the fire of Life and
bring back full health and vitality.
Move through the body's cells to repair and rejuvenate.
May all the right people and circumstances now
come forward for perfect healing.
Whatever medicine, healing agents, doctor's or procedures may
be necessary,
may they now be drawn into our lives and shown to us clearly.
May all that is used, be guided by the Angels of Light.
I know that there is Divine Wisdom in the body that reflects
the perfection
of the Holy Healer—I call that Healer forth now to return this
body to it's radiant natural state of life abundant.
I release my fears to You.
I allow myself to hear and listen to Your voice guiding me onward.
I let go of my anxiety and open my heart to embrace this child.
I realize that I cannot see or know the entire path of myself nor
anyone else.

I surrender now to Higher Wisdom to guide the way for us now.
Thank You for hearing my plea.
Thank You for healing us together.
Amen

## Prayer Before Surgery or Medical Procedure

Dear God, I place myself in Your hands today.
My body and mind belong to You.
I breathe in Your healing love and serenity now and know that
You are healing my mind of all fear and apprehension.
I place Divine Wisdom in charge of this day and of this process.
Angels surround me and lift me up.
Unseen beings of Holy Light guide the hands of every doctor
and nurse.
Radiant Light flows through my veins and enlivens the cells of
my body.
My immune system is now enlivened by Divine Power.
All medicines taken are infused with the purity of the Spirit of
God's love.
The past is over and whatever has come
before this moment is forgiven and released.
This is a new day.
I am opening now to allow the forces of healing to take over
my body.
My mind is focused on serene and compassionate breathing.
There is nothing for me to do but relax into the God-flow.
There is nothing to fear.
There is nothing to resist.
All is unfolding now in a state of perfect grace.
Thank You Lord for taking over.
I let go—I let God.
Amen

*The moment you try to avoid anything, you have to control everything.*
*Let go of avoiding and controlling.*

# Prayer For My Home

God's love fills and surrounds my home.
I am safe here for I am sheltered by the love of God.
My home and all my surroundings are beautiful and supportive
to my own inner-awareness of the comfort and
beauty of the Spirit behind all things.
This is a warm and inviting environment for myself and all those
who enter.
There is always more than enough money to pay the bills and to
sustain my home with all that I need in order to live joyfully and
abundantly.
This is a sacred place and I fill it with the God-vibration
which attracts wonderful people and experiences.
This is a refuge and a sanctuary.
May I find my rest here.
The rooms are filled with the laughter of those I love.
This is the background for many wonderful memories yet to come.
My home reflects the highest and best within me and is a constant
reminder that I am an able, capable and loving person.
The neighborhood in which I live is a loving, safe place.
I love and bless my neighbors and send this blessing out
my front door and into the streets of this town.
There are Angels at the door, on the street corners and in every
home I see.
All darkness is banished and Divine Light protects us all.
There is nothing to fear.

I allow myself to belong here.
I allow myself to have this blessing.
Thank You God that it is so.
Amen

# Entering The Temple

I know that I am safe in God's loving care.
I let go of all concepts I have about myself.
I lay aside my past and future goals.
I rid myself of all mistakes, grievances and faults.
I release what think I want or need in order to be happy.
I unburden myself as I breathe in the cool and gentle air.
It is safe for me to relax and let go for I am in the Temple;
the Secret Place of the Most High.
I am bathed in the glow of a thousand candles.
Angels sing to me songs of peace and love beyond measure.
My heart softens in the love which floods my being.
I am in His presence now and I am safe.
Here, I seek and find the forgiveness that I need.
I turn away from the outer world and all that concerns me there.
Here I am safe to be who I really am.
There is nothing to get and nothing to want.
I am in the presence of all the saints and prophets.
Jesus, Moses, Mary and the Buddha live here,
and I abide with them.
I am washed clean in the living waters.
I am anointed by the Angels.
My spirit is renewed and I am filled with vital energy.
The life force within me grows strong.
My burdens have been lifted from me and I am able to

return to the world with a heart full of compassion and serenity.
Thank You Lord that this is so.
Amen

# Prayer For Our Pets

There is a Divine Spirit in all animals everywhere and
even now they are being blessed by an angel of God.
I place my pets in the care of that angel.
Divine love now enfolds my animal friends and keeps them
safe from all sickness and harm.
I send out my love and appreciation now for their
Companionship and unwavering love.
There is an unbroken bond of communication between us
which supports us both in knowing that we are not alone.
My heart is overflowing.
This is a sacred trust and I gladly accept the responsibility
of this precious and tender life.
I make time for my pet and lovingly groom and care
for him with tenderness and loving-kindness.
I know that right now the consciousness of all human-kind
is shifting to honor the Divinity in all of life,
including these precious creatures.
The world is being transformed into a safe habitat for animals to
live with us in safety, harmony and balance.
We are all able to thrive in the light of God's love.
I devote myself now to not only knowing the truth
of this but also to doing whatever I can to be
a human who is responsible for living in harmony with nature.
I place the animals in the care of God.
May I do no harm.

May I be of help.
Thank You God.
Amen

# Prayer For The Loss Of A Loved One

I open my heart now that I may be healed.
I allow myself to feel the deep emotions which
fill my being and I know that I am not alone in my pain.
There is an angel of mercy and compassion who is beside me now.
It is safe for me to grieve and I know that I am comforted by
the love of God which surrounds me now.
There is no loss except in time and I realize that in
the reality of Spirit I am still one with this person.
Divine comfort fills me and heals my wounded heart.
The grace of God is running my life while I am in mourning.
There is nothing to resist nor rush through for I honor this
sacred cycle of birth, death and rebirth.
All is well in the Universe and I am forever part of all that is.
I let go of our physical relationship and give
thanks that we had this time together on Earth.
I now open up to a relationship of the spirit.
I release this person to their greater and highest good now
as I focus on the essence of our love for one another.
All communication is now heart-communication.
There is no space nor distance in the heart.
I know that my loved one lives on inside me and we are together.
This day I seek and find the comfort of the Divine Mother.
May I be held in the Divine arms.
May I be cradled by the angels.
I rest in God.

May my loved one rest in God as well.
I let go.
I let God.
Thank You Lord.
Amen

## Prayer For Veterans and Soldiers

Blessings on the men and women who have stood up for what is right.

This very day the angels of justice and mercy surround each one of them and bathe them in a divine protective light.

Peace reigns down this day from Heaven.

All is well and every man, woman and child may live in serenity knowing that God is holding the world in His hands.

All those who have been injured or harmed in any way by the tragedy of war are this very moment being healed by Divine Restoration.

All that they need is drawn to them now.

Love, friendship, prosperity, acknowledgment, assistance and health are their Divine Inheritance this very day.

All obstacles to peace and plenty dissolve in the blaze of God's fiery love.

All minds are healed, bodies cared for and hearts mended.

The Holy Spirit now takes every memory of pain and darkness and cuts the cords which bound them to the mind.

Sweet relief is breathed in and all is well.

Praise God for these brave and noble ones who followed their inner-call.

May they be safe from all harm.

May they recover quickly from any and all illness, disease or injury.

May there never be another moment of fighting, violence or injustice on the Earth.

May the need for armies end.
May we learn to love and honor one another.
I now join my thoughts to the Holiest of Holies that my mind
may be cleansed of all anger, resentment and violence.
May peace begin with me.
May it begin now.
Please God, help us to do right.
Help us to see no value in attack or defense.
Thank You God.
Amen

# Body/Food Prayer

God is everywhere present and can heal all things.
God is healing my mind of all judgment and pain
regarding my body and food.
I claim for myself a healthy and loving relationship with my body
and food.
I love my body regardless of its appearance, shape and size and
I am so grateful to it for it serving me so well.
I do not use my body to store emotions nor do I use food to
comfort my pain.
Spirit now harmonizes, balances and restores every cell of my
body as well as my physical, emotional and mental appetites.
I enjoy healthy nutritious foods and release all guilt regarding
eating.
There is nothing to change, fix or manipulate.
There is no need for control, discipline or deprivation.
My appetite is wholesome and regulated by Spirit.
I do not deserve to be punished in any way.
I am at peace with myself and with my sexuality.
It is safe for me to be physically attractive and beautiful.
There is nothing to fear. I am worthy and beautiful and all is well.
I embrace my sensuality and I do not use my body to "get"
anything nor to keep anything or anyone away.
The past is over and no one can hurt nor violate me in any way.
I now love and accept my body for the divine
and precious gift that it is.

May it be used by Spirit to do God's will.
It is forgiven and I am forgiven and we are released together.
I allow myself to have a beautiful, healthy, strong and attractive body.
Praise God for this miraculous healing.
Thank You Jesus for walking with me today.
I am filled with love. And so it is.
Amen

# Blessing Before A Meal

In gratitude and joy we sit in the presence of the Divine
as we join together to celebrate this meal.
This food is infused by the spirit of love and abundance
to nourish our bodies and strengthen us to live.
We are thankful for this chance to come together as family and
friends to acknowledge that which is sacred in the ritual of taking
in sustenance.
May we grow in love here today.
May we open to hear one another.
May our conversation be meaningful and intimate.
May joy find place at this table.
May all feel welcome and at home.
Join with us now Lord as we acknowledge Your presence here
among us.
Thank You for another day together.
Thank You for this life.
Amen

# Prayer For Safe Travel

As I take this journey I send out my loving thoughts before me
to light up the way with happy loving experiences.
There is no time nor place where I am separate from God and
I am on safe and holy ground wherever I go.
All stress, worry and anxiety dissolve as I relax and let go.
My travel is safe and comfortable.
Planes, trains, cars, buses and boats are all the same to God
and I now invite Him to take the helm and lead the way.
My accommodations fill my every need and are just right for me.
The entire Universe is my home for God is with me always.
No one is a stranger to me but only a brother or sister I have yet
to embrace.
My Divine Companion travels with me this day and
I am guided through all things by this Guardian Angel.
The spirit of joy is spread out before me like a carpet that
welcomes me everywhere I go.
I am surrounded by congenial, loving people and my way is
made easy and straight. All is well.
All that is necessary to have a successful and happy trip
is drawn to me by Divine Attraction.
My days are filled with Divine Activity.
There is no need to worry or rush.
I am on God's schedule and all my experiences unfold
according to Divine Timing.
I relax into this truth.

I open my heart and mind to experience the goodness that is all around me.

I let go of control and allow God to take care of every need I may have.

No harm can come to me nor to my companions for the Divine Mother has her loving arms around us now.

I am so grateful for this opportunity to see what God would have me see and to meet those whom God would have me meet.

I embrace the perfection of this glorious and holy day.

I am at home.

I am peaceful and happy.

Thank You God.

Amen

# Prayer For Financial Abundance

There is no lack in God and none in me.

As the Universe is infinite and knows no limits, neither do I.

I am one with all of Life and that Creative Principle of Life creates abundance through and for me.

There is no need to hoard nor squander.

I constantly attract financial prosperity and I am a grateful receiver.

I always have more than enough money to pay my bills, enjoy my life and to contribute and share my wealth with those I love as Spirit directs.

I am not afraid of prosperity and I relinquish all my judgments about money and about wealthy people.

I know that it is God's will that all His children be provided for in every way possible and I will not oppose His will with thoughts or beliefs about struggle and poverty.

Abundance is the most natural law of the world for there are more than enough grains of sand on the beach, stars in the sky and the Universe is forever expanding and making more.

I let go of all past patterns and beliefs about money.

I forgive my parents for any fears I may have learned from them regarding money and prosperity. My mind is now healed.

I allow myself to receive my good now for I am a trustworthy steward with money and know that money is merely a form of energy.

There is nothing good nor bad about money and prosperity—abundance is as natural as breathing in and breathing out.

I allow myself to enjoy saving, spending, investing, tithing, circulating and playing with money. I use money lovingly and joyfully.

I follow the Holy Spirit's inner direction as to what to do with all my finances for I realize that God is the source of my supply regardless of the particular human vessels which He uses to distribute the flow.

Thank You Lord for trusting me with this wonderful supply.

May I do only good with it.

May it bless the world.

Amen

## Prayer For Release From Fear & Anxiety

Dear Lord, I admit that I am afraid and I know that
You are not the author of fear.
From this moment on I let go of terrorizing myself with my
thoughts.
Today I will not condone nor indulge
my own worrying and obsessive negativity.
Today I believe in Your hand upon my shoulders leading and
guiding me through all situations and controlling all outcomes.
I realize I am not alone and I have a Companion Who knows
who I am and what I need. Divine Aid is mine now.
I take a deep breath and surrender my fears into the arms of the
Divine Mother.
Nothing and no one can interfere with the miracles I now claim
for myself and for this situation.
All anxiety, dread and panic dissolve now and
I allow my body to relax and let go.
My shoulders drop, my jaw and forehead relax and all
tension is released into the White Light of Your Divine Love.
My heart is beginning to soften as I release being right about my
fears.
I am an innocent child of God who believes in the
miracles which defy all the laws of this world.
I surrender now into the laws of God.
I will not project my thoughts into the future.
I will not keep repeating my past. My faith is in You God.

I know that You are greater than any person, condition or situation.
I am washed clean in the Living Waters.
It is easy for me to breathe in and breathe out for the Holy Spirit now enters my body and clears my mind of all thoughts which do not bring peace, clarity and calm.
Thank You Lord for the answer to all my problems.
Thank You for walking with me today.
I love You and trust You in all things and in all ways.
Amen

*<u>Strange but often true:</u>*
*The moment you truly release your emotional or psychic attachment to something you want-that thing tends to become irresistibly attracted to you.*

# Prayer For Healing Negativity

Lord, I know that my own cleverness has been used against me.
My intelligence and insights have often brought me pain.
I confess that my past hurts have sometimes hardened me against
love and increased my emotional armor.
This is not how I want to live.
I now let down these defenses.
I let go of being right and quick and clever.
I let go of my observations of what and who is wrong.
I release my cynicism and doubts.
I am now filled with Your holy innocence.
It is safe for me to trust in Your love and protection.
It is safe for me to relax and let go.
I choose from this day on to forgive quickly.
I will no longer do mental reruns of past hurts.
I now choose to think of the Universe as a friendly place.
I choose to notice the good in people and in situations.
I seek a new mind and a new heart.
From this moment on Divine thinking fills my world.
I am attracted to and notice the good all around me.
I am part of that good which lights the Universe.
I now realize that all things are unfolding perfectly for my
highest and best good and I welcome this new life.
Now I am given another chance to live joyfully.
I offer this new self to You God.
Heal me now Father.

Bless me Divine Mother.
Give me wings to fly that my heart may soar.
Amen

# Prayer for Healing a Broken Heart

God, the pain I now feel is deep and its' burden is great.
I keep repeating my thoughts of the past
and going over what happened until I am tormented.
Please heal my mind of the tendency to dwell in yesterday.
Heal my heart of this aching wound.
I know that Your angel of mercy is here beside me now and
I lean on the heavenly shoulder for comfort.
Whatever tears are left are cleansing me and I allow myself to cry
them all.
I allow myself now to move through this process so that I may
be reborn.
I will heal from this and I will love again with Your help.
I am willing to let go of the past as best I can.
May only the blessing of our love remain.
I will not use this as a reason to harden myself nor to withdraw
from life.
I deserve love and happiness. I know that it is God's will for me.
I release this person now to their highest and best good.
I know that as I release my partner, I am released as well.
I cannot move on while holding onto grievances or to the past.
From this moment on I shall increase in love and strength.
My heart is healing and opening up to experience what is next
for me.
There is no delay in God's plan for my life and for my good.
I gratefully allow myself to be guided and led by the Holy Spirit.

Even now the seeds of love are planted and rooted in my heart.
My eyes are opening up to see the new opportunities that are here and now.
I am drawn to that which is for my highest good.
Unseen angels guide my every step, my every thought, my every action.
Nothing good is withheld from me and
I know that I deserve the greatest love of all.
Thank You Divine Spirit for this miraculous healing.
I give myself to You.
Amen.

## Prayer For Healing Loneliness & Isolation

Oh Lord, for too long I have punished myself with this isolation.
I hid myself away from the world and thought I was safe.
I realize that I only hurt myself more by
cutting myself off from the love of others.
I realize that I am never truly alone for You are here beside me.
And now I seek Your presence in the hearts my
brothers and sisters here on Earth.
I now breathe Your loving presence into the silent chambers of
my heart.
I fill the emptiness with my Divine Companion.
There is no lack of people in the world and I
now allow my heart to fill with love for all people everywhere.
I am surrounded by the goodness of humankind.
I let go of thoughts that I am not good enough.
I let go of my judgmental thoughts of others.
Right now Divine Spirit is drawing to me wonderful
loving friends & experiences.
The Universe knows who are the ideal companions for me
and now draws us together.
We find joy in one another's company.
We share life's journey and walk the path together.
We open our hearts to one another's differences and
accept the gift of learning from them.

Thank You Divine Mother and Father that I live in a world filled with limitless possibilities and potential for harmonious relationships.

I open myself now to let people in—it is safe for me to be loved.

I release all unconscious hurts and resistance to people now and I allow myself to reach out to others.

I am no longer afraid of revealing myself.

Serenity, confidence and peace fill me as I now approach the people who are put in my pathway—I reach out my hand now and greet them with love and friendship.

I am a worthwhile person and I deserve to have a life filled with loving companions.

I will do my best to not decide where these people shall come from, what they should look like, what their background or goals should be—

I instead, place my faith in You choosing for me.

In love and gratitude and praise I enter the world.

Praise be to God.

Amen

# Prayer Before A Date

Dear God, I surrender all my thoughts about this date
and about this person to You.
I let go of projecting my goals and needs onto this person
so that I may see who they truly are.
My best self now comes forward and I stand strong in Divine
Confidence.
There is no need for me to be anything other than my real self.
I relax into being exactly who I am and who I am not.
I let go of trying to please, impress or gain approval.
I focus on the joy of getting to know this person and sharing
with them.
I open my heart to seeing who this person really is.
I let go of my judgments.
I release my past experiences of dating and relationships and
am healed.
I let go of any blockages, negative thoughts or cynical nature.
I let go of feeling I am not good enough.
I let go of thinking that others are not good enough.
I know that I am a precious gift of God in whom He is well pleased.
I release all fear. My heart is at peace now. All is well.
Peace and joy are my only goals.
There is nothing to strive for nor to "get".
I do not go on this date alone, but walk with the Holy Spirit.
I call my real self forward now and I relax into this experience.
This is an experience of joy and sharing of two souls.

I speak from my heart with no hidden agendas or goals.
It is safe for me to show up fully and to let my light shine freely.
I am already filled with God's love and I share this light
with all who are near me.
Nothing and no one can ever diminish my inner-light.
Lord, walk with us now so that no matter what the outcome
we will feel happy and at peace.
All now unfolds beautifully and easily according to Your will.
Thank You for this wonderful experience.
May we both be blessed.
Amen

# Preparation Prayer For Sexual Intimacy

Lord, I surrender this most beautiful act to the living spirit of love which radiates through all life.

This sharing with my partner is an act of spirit moving through the flesh.

I take responsibility for my own actions and perceptions here.

I will not use this sharing as a way to hurt or punish myself.

I let go of any feelings of guilt or false beliefs regarding sex.

I fully move into my body and I celebrate and share its beauty and the beauty of my partner.

I let go of my critical mind and judgments
that I may be fully present in my heart.

I allow myself to be open and vulnerable to this person.

I release my thoughts of all past sexual experiences so that I may fully enjoy whatever unexpected pleasures come from the present moment.

I let go of any predetermined outcome or goal and relax into the sharing of physical intimacy with my partner.

May this be a blending of physical, spiritual and mental desires to give and receive pleasure and love.

May this experience be a greater joining of two souls and not a way to hide from one another.

May this be a loving and safe experience for both of us.

May it reflect our inner-selves.

May we deeply surrender to one another.

May we grow closer in love and communication.

May our love come shining through.
Thank You Father Mother God for joining with us now.
Amen

# Prayer For Family Healing

Dear God, I place my family in Your hands now.
These people are so dear and precious to my heart and yet there
are ways in which we have hurt and disappointed one another.
Misunderstandings and fear have built up walls that have kept
our love from coming through as brilliantly as we meant it to.
There are times when we have strayed far from our hearts and
spoken from our pain.
We have attacked and defended and left one another scarred.
Please take all of this past hurt away now.
Bring to the forefront the love that has always been there.
I know that all life is forever bound together in the Divine
and Holy consciousness of God.
My family and I are part of that Divine Mind.
Come into us now.
I now surrender my own wounds from the past and
am willing to see everyone
in a completely different way.
Restore my mind now to Eternal Truth.
I will not dwell upon the mistakes and guilt of those around me.
I will no longer hold onto my own errors.
I forgive myself and I forgive my family.
The past is over and has no power over me.
I feel the eyes of God upon us.
I now claim for myself and for this family a healing of the heart
and mind.

From this moment on the Angels will lift us to highest places in our minds.
Nothing can delay the will of God and I know that
Your will is for our happiness.
We are restored in this Holy Instant of forgiveness.
I breathe in this truth.
I place my faith in the Lord.
Thank You Divine Mother.
Praise the Divine Father.
Amen

## Prayer for Empowered Aging

Dear God, I thank You for bringing me to this place in my life.
So many of my companions did not make it this far and
I sometimes fear that one day I will stand all alone in this world.
I release these fears to You now.
I am at peace with my past and honor the people and
the path that brought me here today.
I am an ageless spirit and I embrace the wisdom of my life
experiences.
I bless this body which I inhabit and fill it with the Holy Breath
of Life.
Each breath I take renews and restores the cells of my body and
dissolves all worry and pain.
My mind is clear and sharp and I am interested in the life all
around me.
I release my body and mind from the past and from any effects
of past hurts.
I am forever an effect of the Divine Ageless Spirit of Wisdom
and Love eternal.
All that remains of my past experience are
the lessons of love given and received.
I harbor no resentments or anger against anyone or anything.
My life begins anew each and every morning.
It is never too late for me to begin anything for I live by the
God-clock.
I am forever in the right place at the right time.
Today is the day—this is the moment.

I am enthusiastic about exactly where I am at this point in my
life and I do not allow the voices of the world to tell me who I
am or what my place is.
I have a purpose that only grows stronger
and more magnificent with each year.
All those who for whom a relationship with me is mutually
beneficial are irresistibly drawn to my side now.
My body and mind know no age.
My face and my body are lit from within
by a full and rich life of love and learning.
I stand here in Your Presence and look out onto the horizon
at all the adventures yet to come.
May I walk in Your Light.
May Your Love enfold me.
May this body be blessed to serve me well.
I have so much yet to give.
Use me Lord.
Amen

# A Prayer For Healing Depression

Lord, somehow my thoughts have sunk into a dark place.
I feel bound and trapped in a cycle of hopelessness and pain.
This is not where I want to be.
I want to feel Your joy in me and in my life.
I want so much to feel myself wrapped in Your Divine Arms.
Come into me now. Heal me and fill me with Your Light.
I willingly release the thoughts and feelings which have
haunted me and driven me to this place.
I do not want them anymore and I banish them from my mind
and heart.
I know that Your Power and Presence can heal all things, even this.
I let go of any attachments I may have to my sadness
for it no longer serves me in any way.
I release the need to be right about my thoughts.
I am an innocent child of Yours and I do not deserve this pain.
I deserve to walk in the sun again.
With Your help all fear is now vanquished and dissipates into
the Light.
From this moment on I claim for myself abundant life and
renewed interest in living.
Whatever thoughts or experiences have brought me into the
dark night-I release them now.
They have no power over me for I stand in Divine Light.
Nothing can touch me or deter me from my right path.
By the power of my word I now claim the joy and happiness

that God has willed to me.
Let nothing and no one come between me and my inner-light.
This is my new beginning Lord.
Thank You for this healing.
Thank You for this moment in time.
I love You and I am willing now to learn to love myself.
Hallelujah, praise God.
Let it be so.
Amen

*Prescription for health:*
*Stop apologizing, hiding or lying about who or what you are or what you feel.*
*If it is physically unsafe to do so, then bide your time in prayer until it is safe.*

# Prayer For Dealing With Rejection

Lord, I feel defeated and discouraged.
I put myself out there and it seems that the result was
hurtful to me and to my pride.
In a moment of vulnerability my tender self was somehow squelched.
In spite of this I know that these feelings are not the truth about me.
The truth about me is grander and greater than any single
experience.
The truth about me is greater than the approval or acceptance
of others.
I will resist the temptation to harbor negativity about myself or
Toward those whom I feel did not want my gift.
I know that there is a reason for everything that occurs in me and
in my world and I accept that this is for my best and highest good.
Another door is opening for me even now.
There are limitless opportunities for my good and I invoke
them now.
My eyes are opening to new possibilities and I am
renewed and strengthened by Divine Spirit.
I know that right now those whom will love and appreciate who
and what I am are on their way to me and I release all past
experience in order to stand ready for their arrival.
I acknowledge myself for having shown up for life and for
participating.
I am so glad that I took the chance.
Thank You for the opportunity to play in the game of life.

I open my heart to learn whatever You would have me learn
from this situation.
I will not use it as a block to my own growth nor
as an excuse to play small in the future.
I am the same one I always was and nothing
can change my beauty and brilliance.
I was created by You just as I am.
I bless and release all participants in this situation to their greater
good and I bless myself for my courage and willingness.
I am lovable, capable and worthy.
Praise God for all that I am,
for all that I have been given.
Amen

## Prayer For Another Person

Dear Lord, I place the life of _____, into your hands.
I know that Your love is filling and surrounding him/her now.
In this moment I claim for _____ a Divine
Intervention and Healing
of all circumstances and I know that my prayer is heard.
I release my will and place this person into Your hands now.
I declare now in Jesus name that _____'s every need is
taken care of in this moment and that his/her Divine Inheritance
is fulfilled.
May the Angels surround and lift _____ up.
May there be an end of pain and a return of joy and peace and
laughter.
May all sorrows be comforted and lifted.
May I be of help in whatever way You guide me to be.
Right now in this very moment every cell of _____'s
body is being infused with the Healing Light of Christ.
Every breath comes easily and restores, soothes, energizes and heals.
They feel this love now.
Any and all sickness, disease or despair vanishes in this Holy
Instant.
All poverty, lack and emotional turmoil cease.
Anger is released—resentments dissipate.
The Holy Mother cradles _____ in Her arms.
The power of the love in my heart gives wings to this prayer
and delivers the healing now.

Nothing can deny the will of God. All is well.
I release this into Divine Hands and trust that all outcomes are right.
So it is. And so I let it be.
Hallelujah.
Amen

# Prayer For Releasing Addictions

Dear Lord, I feel so out of control and insane.
I do not know who I am anymore and I have lost my way
back to a safe harbor.
I feel so guilty and ashamed and yet I know that You
have not turned Your face from me.
I want so much to be released from this bondage.
I want to live again.
I need to feel Your forgiveness wash over me—
to cleanse me of this illness, of this despair and longing.
I claim a miracle for myself now.
I claim my Divine Inheritance.
I know that I am still Your child and that Your power is flowing
through my body and mind even now.
I am being restored by the power of Your grace.
I am not alone.
In truth I am not lost.
I am being healed by Divine Love.
My life begins anew and the past is washed away.
My desires are now transforming and I want only
what is wholesome, helpful and right.
I am becoming relaxed and peaceful inside.
God has heard my call.
I am safe from all harm.
Thank You God.
Amen

# Holiday Prayer

Dear God, I surrender all my thoughts
and expectations about this holy season to You.
I release myself and my loved ones from my own agenda and
goals so that we may more fully embrace what You would have
us experience.
May we all be blessed by a greater experience of mindfulness,
serenity and love.
I now choose to remember what is truly important.
There is no need to rush, hurry or to do everything exactly right-
I am enough just as I am.
Gifts, cooking, decorating, cards and parties are wonderful
but merely surface manifestations of an inner-experience.
Let me not forget this.
It is okay for things to be messier than usual.
It is okay if I do not get everything done.
The perfection of this season is not in outer things,
but rather in the Light that is within me now.
May my heart open wide to all the miracles that
are unfolding in my life this very moment.
May I see the angels that surround me.
May I be an angel for someone else.
Thank You Lord.
Amen

# New Year Prayer

Dear Lord, I stand here at the threshold of a new year.
The past is fading behind,
and the future is a bright light just ahead.
I take a moment now to breathe in the Holy Present.
Stand with me now—be the Guide Who clears my mind and opens my heart.
I gently and gratefully release the year gone by.
I bless it all: the good and the bad, the pain and the joy,
the teachers and the lessons learned.
It is over now and only the love remains.
The year before me is yet a blank page -
Write Your name on it Dear Lord.
Fill each day with your Holy Presence.
Make me a child of Light.
This is who I am.
This is why I came.
My mind is filled with Holy Spirit Power.
The road is set before me.
The path made straight.
From this moment on I shall never walk alone.
Praise God for this new year, this new day, this new life.
Amen

# Chapter Six

## The Exercises

*"Nothing in the world can take the place of persistence. Talent will not;
nothing is more common than unsuccessful individuals with talent.
Genius will not; unrewarded genius is almost a proverb. Education
will not; the world is full of educated derelicts. Persistence and determi-
nation alone are omnipotent>"*

Calvin Coolidge

God can help us only if we are willing to change. It is necessary for us to look at ourselves and grow from the investigation. Therefore, it is very helpful to find various ways to do our inner work. This section of exercises presents some of the ways we can create those inner changes.

If we do not work on our own healing, the universe sends us countless "teachers" who will come to show us where we are stuck. They will look like obstacles, some will even look like enemies. In truth, they are here to bring up our unhealed issues so that we can release them. As long as we are in denial about our own issues, we cannot have them removed. What stays hidden has a way of running the show from behind the scenes, ruining situation after situation until we finally face the problem within.

Many of us walk around with psychic, emotional "buttons" covering up our real essence. When people push these buttons through their words or actions, it feels like they are putting their hands in our open wounds. We tend to want to get rid of those people or these situations. Sometimes we are just praying to meet people who have no fingers. That is not God's plan for our healing. God heals us by sending people with great big fat fingers. They can't seem to help constantly pushing all our buttons as a way of saying, "isn't it about time you healed this issue?" By doing our inner work, we open up to God removing these buttons so that we can live more joyful, happy lives without having to avoid or control everyone and everything outside of us.

Another problem many of us have, is that we pray and then block the answers when they come. At other times, we have not prepared ourselves as the vessels to receive the blessing. Also, we can get so caught up in our busy daily lives, that we lose sight of why we are running around doing so much. We may have started out with great intentions, but now we are so busy our real intention has been lost in an endless "to do" list.

By doing the exercises that follow, you will have a way to stay focused on what is most important to you and will have a chance to align yourself with thoughts that will support you in living at your highest and best on a more consistent basis.

The exercises are simple and self-explanatory, but in several cases, I have given examples to make it clear. I have not gone into great detail about the purposes of the exercises, because I believe that it will be self-evident when you do them. What is most powerful about them comes over time. Please do return to this section of the book on a regular basis once you have filled it out. I think that you will find this part of the book enlightening and quite enjoyable. In time it will strengthen your spirit and be like a cool drink of water on a hot day.

WHO IS A BLESSING IN YOUR LIFE?
WHEN DID YOU LAST TELL
THEM SO?
TELL THEM NOW.

*"Prayer does something to the mind of the one praying. It does not do anything to God. The Eternal Gift is always made. The Gift of God is the Nature of God, the Eternal Givingness. God cannot help making the gift, because GOD IS THE GIFT. We do not have to pray God to be God. God is God. Jesus revealed the nature of the Divine Being by his personal embodiment of the Divine Nature.*
*He said, "As ye believe, it shall be done unto you."*

Ernest Holmes, The Science of Mind

### The Personal Prayer

I have written dozens of prayers in this book covering a variety of topics that I hope will soothe and restore your soul. Ultimately, of course, you must make your own prayer requests known to God. We are told to ask, to seek, to knock on God's door daily. Therefore I have created this space for you to write your own prayer requests so that you may see them each day as a reminder to place these matters in the hands of God.

Your Personal Prayer is you claiming God's good in order to focus on possibilities on a daily basis rather than focusing on limitations and what is not working. This is the place to write down your heart's desires and make them known to God and to your higher self. Once stated, we release these desires to the will of God. That will is for our highest and best good. We should try not get attached to particular results. We are simply inviting God to enter into our lives by intimately sharing with Him what is in our hearts.

**Example:**

**The Personal Prayer:**

Dear God, These are my prayers needs—I am willing to grow into the space to accept this now or, if it is not for my highest good, to be released from the desire. May God's Will be done and may I have deep peace regarding these ideas and goals.

An increase in peace of mind and a compassionate heart for those whom I do not agree with, safety for my child and for her school and all the other children and teachers there, greater intimacy with my husband, patience in teaching my children, peace & acceptance regarding food and my body, a healthy stable relationship with money and financial freedom, joy and success in my work,, a wonderful vacation this summer with the family, an peaceful end to all wars now, healing for my diabetes, a forgiven relationship with my ex-husband, a new beautiful & reliable car, food & shelter for the homeless, personal courage to go for my dreams.

I surrender all these thoughts and desires to the Divine Master.
May the good manifest easily and be irresistibly drawn to me
in Divine Right order and timing for the highest
good of all concerned.
Thank You God.
Amen

## My Personal Prayer

Dear God, These are my prayers needs—I am willing to grow into the space to accept this now or, if it is not for my highest good, to be released from the desire. May God's Will be done and may I have deep peace regarding these ideas and goals.

_____
_____
_____
_____
_____
_____
_____
_____
_____
_____
_____
_____
_____
_____
_____
_____
_____
_____
_____

I surrender all these thoughts and desires to the Divine Master.
May the good manifest easily and be irresistibly drawn to me
in Divine Right order and timing for the highest
good of all concerned.
Thank You God.
Amen

*"An aim in life is the only fortune worth finding."*

Jacqueline Kennedy Onassis

*"Believe, when you are most unhappy, that there is something*
*for you to do in the world. So long as you can sweeten*
*another's pain, life is not in vain."*

Helen Keller

## Mission Statement:

Your mission is your intention for who you choose to be while here on Earth. Ultimately, it is your life purpose. Take time to consider this. Deep inside you is the answer. It is important to remember that it is meant to use your time, talents and abilities in a way that is deeply satisfying and personally rewarding although it may not be the particular career that you have. It is bigger than a job description or a resume'. It is not contingent on external circumstances or permission from others.

## Mission Roles:

Your mission roles are the way that you participate in living out your life's purpose. They are the various roles that you have in life. As you assign each role its' real significance in the bigger plan for your life, your daily activities are infused with greater purpose and meaning.

## Example:

## My Mission Statement:

My mission is to manifest the highest vision possible for myself by letting God use me as an instrument of love and healing. To be a kind, compassionate, loving and joyful human being. To intimately join with others in love and fellowship. To be known and loved deeply-to love and know others deeply.

**Mission Roles:**

**I am a Child of God**—I love and honor God 1st through daily prayer, meditation and reading spiritual writings.

**I am a Mate**—I love, respect and listen to my lover and am a loving and giving mate, I share of myself and my life and include his life—I make time for us.

**I am a Family Member**—I stay in contact with my family and let them know I care—I call, write and visit

**I am a Businessman**—I let God run my business and I follow the lead He gives me in my prayers and meditations—I pay the bills on time, tithe and allow others to contribute their time and talents to my business.

Etc, etc.

**My Mission Statement:**

_____
_____
_____
_____
_____
_____
_____
_____
_____
_____
_____
_____
_____
_____
_____
_____
_____
_____
_____
_____
_____
_____
_____
_____
_____
_____
_____
_____
_____

_____
_____
_____
_____
_____

**My Mission Roles:**

_____
_____
_____
_____
_____
_____
_____
_____
_____
_____
_____
_____
_____
_____
_____
_____
_____
_____
_____
_____
_____
_____
_____

*"If you keep on saying things are going to be bad,
you have a good chance of being a prophet."*

Isaac Bashevis Singer

**Affirmations and Spiritual Reminders:** Many of us have a daily inner-dialogue that is not particularly uplifting. The affirmative statements (or affirmations) which follow are here to assist you in keeping your thoughts as high and positive as possible each day. I hope they will inspire you to write your own affirmations about the issues that are in your life today. Remember, your words are very powerful so choose them carefully.

I open myself to this new day-
I do not know what is going to happen and so
I allow Divine Spirit to unfold all things perfectly.
Divine Activity fills my day and runs my life.
Today I remember to praise and acknowledge
the people in my life. I am a grateful child of God today.
My body is strong, healthy and fit.
The good that I seek is now seeking me.
Thank You God for manifesting the perfect
outcome in every area of my life.
I am available for miracles.
I am healed by the love I give.
This is an abundant universe and I am open to receive my good.
I am an instrument of Divine Love and Healing.
I am a beautiful person inside and out.
I love myself fully and freely today.
I allow myself to love all people today.
I am always in the right place at the right time.
I am surrounded by angels and filled with the grace of God.
I am always safe, loved and supported.

## Affirmations and Spiritual Reminders

This page is for writing your own affirmations and spiritual reminders

_____

_____
_____
_____
_____
_____
_____
_____
_____
_____
_____
_____
_____
_____
_____
_____
_____
_____
_____
_____
_____
_____
_____
_____
_____
_____
_____
_____
_____

**Prayers for Others & Gratitude List**

On the following page you will find a space to write the names of loved ones that you would like to remember in your daily prayers. I think of this as my "prayer circle" and imagine these people encircled in the light of Divine love and blessings. You may choose to simply write their names or you may want to write beside their name their particular prayer needs.

**Example:**

Caroline—healing of cancer and ease in her medical process.
Stanley—his right work

A gratitude list is a wonderful place to acknowledge the good that is in your life right now. Some people use this list as a place to record answers to prayer requests made in the past or simply as a place to gently remind them of the many blessings that are here and now. We tend to be able to very quickly name everything that is not working or that has gone wrong—it is in these times that we must have as easily accessible a list of the good that has manifested. A grateful heart is a welcoming place for miracles.

**Example:**

My health, my beautiful home, good friends like Zan & Jeannie, a great family, work I love, that weekend in Arizona, etc.

**Prayers For Others: List the people you are praying for**

_____

_____

_____

_____

_____

_____

_____

_____

_____

_____

_____

_____

_____

_____

_____

_____

_____

_____

_____

_____

_____

_____

_____

_____

_____

_____

_____

_____

_____

_____

_____

_____

_____

_____

**Gratitude: Make a list of what you are grateful for**

_____

_____

_____

_____

_____

_____

_____

_____

_____

_____

_____

_____

_____

_____

_____

_____

_____

_____

_____

_____

_____

_____

_____

## The Healing Process

Self-examination and inquiry into our thoughts is the frontier for transforming our lives. Truly we are transformed by the renewing of our minds. This healing is not a matter of thinking only positive thoughts—you'll have millions of thoughts in a day. Everyone has negative thoughts, but you don't have to set the table and invite them to dinner. When you are disturbed by something, stop and ask yourself, "Is this thought high enough for the child of God?" If it's not, then banish it from your mind and send it to the nothingness from whence it came. Try the process below when you recognize that your thoughts are not bringing you peace.

## Questions for the healing process:

- Is this thought the real, honest truth, and do I want to continue to hold onto it?
- Who am I not forgiving?
- Am I punishing myself or another person with these thoughts?
- What does my judgment cost me?
- Is this thought one that I really want to believe?
- How does this thought make me feel?
- What's my payoff in feeling this way?
- Do I want to continue to feel this way?
- In this situation, would I rather be right or happy?
- How do I want to feel?
- What is the highest most loving thought that I could think that would help me feel the way I want?
- Am I willing to have God replace my thoughts with His?

REMEMBER TO:
SLOW DOWN
BREATHE
RELAX
LET GO

**Agreements For More Joyful Living**—read and sign below if this feels right to you. You may want to remove this page place it where you can see it often.

- I take 100% responsibility for my own life, happiness, healing and what I get out of each day and every experience. I do not expect others to fix me or make me happy.
- I agree to love and forgive myself **no matter what!**
- I agree to do whatever it takes to stay centered and clear.
- I agree to stop punishing myself or expecting myself to be perfect.
- I take responsibility for communicating my feelings appropriately.
- I commit to daily spiritual renewal through conscious contact with God in whatever way works best for me.
- I agree to communicate when something is not working for me.
- I do not have to communicate if doing so is unsafe or would do harm to me or to another person. I seek divine guidance regarding appropriateness.
- I will express my love and gratitude to those around me whenever I can.
- I agree to ask for help when I need it. I let go of expecting people to read my mind or know what I want and need.
- I release my loved ones from my expectations that they will meet those wants and needs once I have communicated them. I will let God choose who helps and who does not—without keeping score.
- I agree to communicate my feelings, as best I can, without attack or blame.
- I will help others, as best I can, without taking responsibility for their lives, happiness or experiences.
- I release others from participating in my self-destructive patterns.
- I release myself from participating in the self-destructive patterns of others.

- I agree to keep a positive mental attitude.
- I agree to learn with joy and to trust the process.
- I will say "no" without feeling guilty.
- I will allow others to support me. I do not have to do everything myself.

_____

*Signature*

# Chapter Seven

## Reflections on Life

*"Let not your heart be troubled, neither let it be afraid."*

John 14:27

# WHY BOTHER?

Perhaps the greatest and most insidious challenge that we face in trying to live an exciting and involving life is resisting the evil temptation to think, "why bother?" This is done with such subtlety that it steals away our dreams bit by bit. It is the thought that "it doesn't really matter...who cares?...it doesn't really bother me...no one will notice...what difference will it really make anyhow?"

It is so much easier to spend all our time in the areas of life that show easier or more immediate results. It's so satisfying to see something physical; the car is washed, the papers are typed, the child is fed, the bills are paid—all extremely important things that need to be done and that show immediate gratification. It is perhaps more difficult to do the things which may only show long-term results or perhaps only inner-results which cannot be seen at all by physical eyes.

Dreams are like any other living thing, they prosper from our attention. Attention is the most powerful energy in the Universe. Whatever gets our attention feeds on it and grows. Therefore, if we even give a tiny bit of attention to our dreams; just one tiny baby step, it begins to grow and have movement.

What are your dreams? A happy healthy family? A particular gift you have to give? A loving relationship? A community that is supportive and nurturing? I am sure you have many dreams—some have come true, some are in process and others are gathering dust, but whatever they are, keep walking onward toward them. Getting started is the easy part—even the first step is not such a big deal. The challenge comes from following through even when the initial enthusiasm dies down. The people who achieve their dreams are the ones who make it past the ambiguousness of "why bother?"

# LOVE AND PASSION

In my 20's, I thought that love and passion went hand-in-hand. I held very passionate beliefs about so many things and I thought that it was one of my greatest qualities. As I have matured and gained life experience, I now see that passion and love are two very different things. Many of my greatest mistakes were acted out with great passion and focus. There is a huge difference in speaking passionately about something and speaking lovingly about the very same thing. Passionate communication can bring up great emotion in other people, but just as often it can bring up passionate opposition. I have seen this in my own life. The world changes for the better not so much through passionate debate as from open discourse.

I have experienced the results that come from speaking passionately with the absolute conviction that I am fully in my truth and felt the temporary rush of having made my point, only to then be followed by a strange emptiness. I understand why now—passion often has no humility or an open mind. Speaking with love from a centered place tends to entertain other possibilities. What is most amazing about this is that it creates a context in which you are more likely to be heard. Still, it is not always so easy for me to put this knowledge into practice, yet this much I have learned, you can stand up for what you believe in from a place that does not attack nor diminish others. No matter what is at stake, no matter what the situation, the person with an open heart ultimately carries the greatest strength.

# WHEN SOMEONE IS IN PAIN

A friend of mine coined the phrase "New Age Nausea" which is the tendency among some people to reduce everything down to trite sayings and pat answers. Often the nicest people resort to these tactics when a subject makes them uncomfortable or they don't want to think too deeply about what someone may actually be feeling or going through.

Well-meaning people who are uncomfortable with their own pain or shadow-side will often want to turn away when another person reveals theirs. We may not have their answers, but we can at least invoke Divine Aid for them.

The true mystics understand that the Universe itself is constantly evolving and unfolding and that nothing as complex as a human life can be neatly summed up with a sound-byte. Real growth comes from deep listening, empathy, compassion and the humility to know that we cannot possibly have an answer for someone else. We show our own ignorance when we dismiss and invalidate others with a quick, "have a positive attitude—change your thoughts—look on the bright side." One of the most healing positions that we can take is one of compassionate listening without interruption or unsolicited advice. Words alone do not always heal. Love can. Every time you dismiss someone's feelings or their experience what you tend to do is make them defend themselves all the more. You prove to them that you do not understand what they are going through. To listen deeply to another person's pain, not with the intention to respond, but rather to really understand, is a beautiful gift to give to someone.

Today could be a day of listening with an open heart and mind. Whoever you speak with today, try slowing down your automatic reaction to respond and ask yourself, "what do they need from me now—love or advice?"

# THE MYSTICAL LIFE

Perhaps you are like me in that you tell yourself that you would live a more spiritual life if there were more time or opportunity for spiritual practice. I have found this thought to be a trick of my mind. Daily life itself is our spiritual practice when properly understood. It is important to realize that we need not wear robes or beads or sit in the lotus position to be in a meditative state of grace. Real meditation is simply awareness and concentration.

Personally, I love religious "drag." I love all the outer manifestations of prayer shawls, candles, incense, yoga asanas, music, chimes, waterfalls and the rituals that go with them. Yet, these are simply the outer reflections of an inner experience, they are not the thing itself. The map is not the land, it merely shows the way. You can be a holy woman or man in your daily activities right now.

Today, think of your home as a holy shrine, a monastery, a temple or an ashram. Realize that you are here to serve God by serving God's children. From this point of view everything that you do becomes a sacred act—you need not change any of your normal daily activities. Everything becomes an act of love. Now you do not serve your wife, husband, lover, child or parent…you serve the Divine Beloved. You are not cooking for yourself, you are cooking for the Christ which dwells within you. You are not merely having sex…you are joining with the divine being who dwells within your lover. Every dish that is washed is a ritual of concentration and has meaning—the meaning is love. You may be living in a castle and still be Divinely simple with this way of thinking. You merely caretake what belongs to God now. This is the life of the mystic. Try it for a day and watch how your mood changes.

# ON ACHIEVEMENT

The human heart and mind have a deep desire to express their own uniqueness in the world. Each of us wants to feel that we have made a difference in the lives of those we care about. We sleep a little sounder knowing that today we accomplished something good and personally meaningful. This is a good thing. It is moral, right and noble. However, the desire to achieve becomes perverted when we think that our achievements define who we are and establish our worth.

A newborn baby does nothing—yet is it not totally loved and lovable? Pets can give very little on a purely practical level and yet their worth is often beyond measure. The reason that we so love babies and animals is not for what they do, but rather for who they already are; not for their achievements, but for their essence. The same is true of each one of us now regardless of our age. The greatest achievement there can be is to be totally you—just as God created you.

God knows your strengths and weaknesses and loves you all the more. We are not held back by anything so much as by running around trying to make ourselves worthy, lovable and perfect. To deeply relax into the truth that God within you can and will guide you in all that you can and should do this day, is the way to assure an effortless day of accomplishment. Do this and you will sleep like a baby tonight.

"God, I now realize that You love me even in my darkest hours and in spite of any mistakes I have made. Thank You for the gift of Your grace in my life. Help me to relax into my true nature. From this moment on I let go of my self-condemnation. I know that You made me just the way I am and I am grateful to be me. Amen."

# CRAZY WONDERFUL YOU

Are you the weird one? The misfit? The one who is different? It wouldn't surprise me. Most people who are deeply interested in the life of spirit march to a different drummer. You might be the one the whole family discusses in bewilderment, "you know how he/she is." Every family has at least one-you're probably it. The sensitive people are usually the ones who end up expressing all the unexpressed emotions of the family. Others may poke you with emotional sticks until you finally blow up and then they'll look at you in horror and say, "You're such a hysteric! What's wrong with you? Can't you ever just let anything go?"

Well, that's the point actually, learning to let it all go with peace and grace. That is what meditation and the life of spirit is all about. To choose peace even when *they started it*. To let go of trying to get other people to wake up and be conscious. To let go of what other people think and be true to yourself even when it seems the whole world is against you, without defensiveness or anger. Do you think anyone who ever lived a life of greatness and contribution ever gave a hoot about what the committee's final vote was? Living a life in which you are true to your own Inner-Voice can be very difficult, but not as difficult as living a life run by the standards of others.

This is it. This is your life. It doesn't matter what God has directed other's to do-what is God telling you? You are unique and no one can do what you came here to do. Somewhere someone wants to hear your voice and what you have to say; someone wants to receive what you have to give. Doesn't it make sense to give your gift where it will be most enthusiastically received and used?

# EARTH UNIVERSITY

Everyone we see is a mirror-we either like the reflection or we don't. If you are having a problem with someone, ask yourself, "What is the reflection that I do not like?" It doesn't mean that they are doing something that you do or would do, it may mean that they are doing something that at some level you wish you could do or get away with.

Perhaps you have a problem with a co-worker because they don't work as hard as you but they get all the credit and freedom. This is so common, it is a cliché. You run around trying to please the boss or whoever, not really every doing what you want to do, coming from sacrifice or moral superiority and it pisses you off that someone who is living as they choose seems to be having all the fun and getting all the breaks.

In times of great stress or challenge, we are surrounded by angels and teachers. Angels come to perform miracles of healing, restoration and grace and to give the message of God's love. The teachers come to push us kicking and screaming to the next level of growth and understanding. The teachers are usually the people who tell us "no" when there is every reason in the world for them to say "yes." They are the ones who seem to be deliberately against us, or hurting us, or keeping us from having what we want. It is at these times that we see what we're made of and how little patience we still have. Luckily, we are buffered from some of the harshness of the cold hard look in the mirror of our own ego's by the angels. So, if you are in the midst of a trial today, look for the angels, focus on them…and whoever is pushing your buttons, think of them as the toughest professor you ever had, some-one who is helping you to master an incredibly difficult course at Earth University. You are a graduate student at EU.

# BEING A REAL NOBODY

Sometimes people will ask me how it is possible to stop noticing the behavior of other people-how it is possible to stop focusing on the errors of the world. In truth, it is the easiest thing in the world. What is difficult, what is exhaustingly difficult, is the constant attention to the outer world-to notice whether it is pleasing you or displeasing you. This is the real difficulty, but we have been trained to live difficult lives and call them easy.

See how easy it is to breathe when you do not think about it. Each breath just comes and goes with the next one coming right after. No struggle, no effort, no attention at all. It simply is there and is natural to the system. But, fear stops the breath jus as it stops full and free living. How tiring it would be to have to force each breath in and out all day long. Just as exhausting as constant attention to what everyone is doing right and what everyone is doing wrong. Our greatest fear is just to "be" and to let others be.

Quiet yourself now. Stop yourself. Stop narrating your story in your mind. Stop telling it now. It is not interesting anymore and does not serve you in any positive way. It only serves to keep you small. Stop reporting what "they" are doing or not doing. There is nothing more boring than constantly re-telling the past. What is interesting, is what is happening inside you right now. That is the real story, the real drama. The addiction to being somebody, to making ourselves into something, to becoming more has cost us all peace and serenity. Break the addiction by no longer feeding the beast with the story. What will emerge is the greatest story every told. Refuse to support others in staying stuck in their story. Refuse to put on the worldly suit this week. Choose to be nobody in particular, so that the real you can emerge.

*Give up criticizing yourself
and your life.
God created you just as you are.
There is nothing wrong with you.
You deserve to live and be happy.*

# ROCK MY WORLD

The Federal Express man stood at my front door looking past me at what catches most people's eye first-on my bookshelf is a beautiful autographed picture of Oprah Winfrey on which she wrote, "Best wishes in teaching miracles! Oprah Winfrey." He wanted to know what it said. I told him. Then he wanted to know how I taught miracles. (I give lectures about spirituality and the miracle of God's love on earth.)

Well, of course he was in a big hurry and wanted to know the one thing he needed to know if life to "make it"…in one sentence. Well, my mind was racing. What should I tell him? That love is the answer? That every choice is one between love and fear? To have faith? To surrender to God?

What I heard myself saying was this, "If you want to be happy in life, no matter what happens, you must give up your attachments." I wasn't really sure why I said that even while I was saying it. Later, as I thought more and more about it, I realized again how much easier life would be for all of us if we could just keep that thought in the forefront of our minds at all times. Imagine how effortless life would be.

But, what really haunted me about that exchange was the tragedy of the times we live in which is this: we want a sound-byte for everything, even for the most important questions that we will every ask, for the most meaning-ful situations that will ever confront us-we want someone to rock our world within 5 minutes and if it takes longer-we move on. There is little respect for the process of discovery itself. Then we wonder why we just can't seem to find what we're looking for…usually we rushed past it. It's time to slow down the monkey mind. Life is discovered one moment at a time.

# FOLLOWING THE LIGHT

There is a new movement afoot in this country. There are people of serious intent who have stopped identifying themselves as Christians and have started calling themselves "followers of Christ." To be a follower of Christ is to try to be more like Christ, to actually do what he said. Remember when he cried out, "Why call ye me Lord, Lord, and do not the things I say?"

For many years I would look at the kind of everyday suffering and unkindness that takes place in the world, the kind that we just accept as being inevitable and I would get so upset-shouting to people, "It doesn't have to be this way! It's only because we allow it to happen. We could choose that it be different and then change it." Well, I am not so sure about that anymore. Maybe this is just the way it is **for now**.

Oddly enough, I feel far less bitter and cynical now than I did when I had great hope for the world. When I thought things should be different it made me harder and angrier, more disappointed in myself and in others. Now I realize that the real miracle of life is choosing to focus on love even in an often unloving world. I have more compassion now. To focus on goodness and beauty when people are acting in such a brutal and ugly way; to forgive myself, the world and others for our imperfections-this is what Jesus taught. He never told us to save the world. He did what he personally could to feed the people, to heal them and to help all who came, yet his real teachings were about love and forgiveness in the face of a world that marches onward into fear and attack. He did not ask the world to change but rather taught that *we* must change. This is what it means to follow Christ. We do what we can to be more loving even in the face of lovelessness. We help whoever and wherever we can without fear or worry.

# WHAT'S YOUR PROBLEM?

There is a tendency among many of us to bitterly complain and worry over problems that other people would love to have. You know the kind, "the printer messed up the invitations, the car is in the shop, so-and-so is late, my co-worker is hard to get along with, my family is not supportive, the remodel is taking too long." Nuisances? Yes! Annoying? Yes! Real problems? Well, that is debatable.

Generally speaking, I would guess that the poorest person reading this book has more than many of the people living on the earth today. 35,000 or more people die every day of starvation. Mothers watch their children literally starve to death before their eyes. Hurricanes, earthquakes, bombs, violence and disease rage across the world every single day. Most of us have so much to be thankful for-a bed to sleep in, a place to shower, food to eat, a country in which we can pretty much go where we want and say what we think.

In fact, it is quite possible right now that the problem that you are facing is the best one you've ever had. Perhaps 10 years ago you longed to have a problem like this one. Even when I have car problems now I think back to the many, many years that I walked and took the bus. If you are having problems in your business, perhaps you can think back to the days when you worked for someone who treated you badly.

Since what we focus on tends to increase, doesn't it make sense to shut up about what is going wrong, about what we are worried about or afraid of, and instead start blessing what is going right? Make this a week of gratitude for all that is happening in your life today-it is the 1st step in moving out of the problem and into the solution. Even if you are sick or heart-broken, do your best to soften your heart and relax into what is. Breathe.

# BASIC REMINDERS

After many years of study, I still find that I never outgrow the basic ideas of metaphysics. No matter how advanced the student there is still a deep need for a foundation which never changes. So, in no particular order, here are some basics:

Every thought or action is a choice between love or fear.

We are not victims of the world or of other people, but are often victimized by our own thinking.

We alone are responsible for our thoughts and can consciously choose to think more loving positive thoughts.

It is done unto us as we believe, not as we hope or wish.

Wishy-washy unclear thoughts create wishy-washy unclear results.

Forgiveness is always a gift to yourself and is not giving approval to another person's harmful behavior.

The world we see is the one we project-there is no such thing as an objective world. The way we choose to look at something affects and determines the outcome.

Thought is the most powerful creative force in the Universe. Life was created from God's thought. The most powerful thought is always the most loving thought.

Nothing and no one outside of you can take away your freedom to choose what you want to think.

Whatever you focus on tends to grow and increase.

# LAUGHING ALL THE WAY

Joy and laughter can get you through the darkest times. This is one of the keys to longevity and health. Life is far too serious to be taken so seriously. In my work, every day brings news of someone in heartache, someone sick, someone dying, someone losing everything-it goes on and on. It is too heartbreaking to drink it all in every time.

The authentic life is one in which we can be crying one moment and laughing the next. Now, this is uncomfortable for people who want to be emotionally stable, but what's so great about being emotionally stable? Nothing here is stable. Every aspect of the physical universe is totally unstable because everything is always changing. The nature of energy is to be in motion.

Most people take themselves and their lives far too seriously. If at all possible I laugh my way wherever I am going. Sometimes I have laughed with someone who was critically ill but who was able to see the ridiculousness of life, occurring within it's most profound moments. I am not sure whether laughter heals the body, but I know that it heals the mind and heart.

To be light and joyful does not exclude having a reverence for life. Have you ever noticed how joyful deeply spiritual people are even when they are in the midst of heartbreak or struggle? Doesn't the Dalai Lama usually have a big beautiful silly grin on his face? Wasn't there always a twinkle in the eye of Mother Teresa? When we realize that death is perfectly safe and that we'll survive it-why walk around in constant fear? Life is meant to be enjoyed.

# SPIRITUAL MATURITY

To begin to observe ourselves, our minds, our thoughts, reactions, and what is happening in our bodies without judgement or "good/bad" categorizing is the start of spiritual maturity. This is what it means to "be here now". Emotions are so fleeting when we do not become attached to them, making them right or wrong or justifying them. There is no need to be stuck in our feelings. Self-reflection is the way of the sage.

The more I observe myself in this way, the more compassion I have for myself and for others. Even though it may not necessarily change my actions in the moment, it keeps me from hanging on to an experience after it is over. This is true freedom.

When we see how out of control our own reactions and thoughts are, it is easier to let go of the "why" other people do and say the things that they do. The mind that judges and evaluates is totally insane in it's reasoning and following that mind-set can only lead to pain and frustration.

Imagine how peaceful you would feel if you just allowed yourself to be who and what you are, without defensiveness or justification? What if you trusted yourself? What if you stopped doubting and second-guessing your own inner-direction? What if you allowed other people to be who they are without your correction or helpful criticisms? What if you resolved to do no harm to yourself or another ever again? What if you simply allowed all things to be as they are without pushing them away or chasing after endless goals? What if you awoke to the present moment just as it is and just as it is not?

If you think someone is stopping you from living this way, ask yourself, what is your payoff in having them be there? Can you forgive them? Can you forgive yourself? We are all doing the best we can.

# ON DEATH

I have visited quite a few bedsides of people who were preparing to exit this physical realm. As a minister and teacher, they usually want to tell me what they have learned on their journey here, how they feel about leaving, and to have me give them some words of reassurance. It is an honor to be part of their process and it has taught me a lot about the eternal nature of life and spirit.

I believe that our real self goes on and on forever. This physical life is just a blip on the screen of our real lives, which are limitless. I think of this life as a classroom where we come to learn lessons in loving. Some of us have bigger, more difficult lessons than others, but the purpose is the same-to learn to love and let go.

When someone is dying, everyone comes to say that final "I love you". That is wonderful. There is so much love in those rooms. But, I think that that is not necessarily what the person needs to hear most. By the time we get to this last phase of the trip it is rather obvious how much we are loved.

What I find myself telling people in those situations is this, "everything is okay now, the people here will miss you, but they'll be okay, you did a great job. You can go whenever you're ready." This is what we long to hear most...that we did not waste our time here on earth. We want to know that "it is accomplished" so that we can move on feeling complete. I tell them, "you were the best Mark anyone could have ever wanted—mistakes and all. No one could have been the Mark that you were." This is what I believe God tells us when we arrive on the other side. "Thanks for being the you I created. Thanks for being exactly the way you were, and exactly the way you were not. I have enjoyed every moment of your journey. Good job my child. Come right in."

# *Suggested Readings*

*A Return to Love, Illuminata, Healing the Soul of America, Enchanted Love, A Woman's Worth* by Marianne Williamson

*Chicken Soup For The Teenage Soul* by Kimberly Kirberger, Jack Canfield, Mark Victor Hanson

*Teen Love* by Kimberly Kirberger

*The 7 Habits of Highly Effective People* by Steven Covey

*How To Heal Your Life* by Louise Hay

*The Four Agreements, The Mastery of Love* by Don Miguel Ruiz

*The Dynamic Laws of Prosperity* by Catherine Ponder

*The Rights of The Dying* by David Kessler

*The Tao of Leadership* by John Heider

*The Path* by Laurie Beth Jones

The Future of Love by Daphne Rose Kingma
*What You Think Of Me Is None Of My Business* by Terry Cole-Whittaker

*Building Your Field of Dreams* by Mary Manin Morrissey

*A Course In Miracles* © The Foundation For Inner Peace

*The Science of Mind* by Ernest Holmes

*Spiritual Journeys Along The Yellow Brick Road* by Darren Main

*17 Ways To Eat A Mango* by Joshua Kadison

*Shortcuts to Bliss* by Jonathan Robinson

*Welcome to the World Baby Girl, Fried Green Tomatoes at the Whistle Stop Café* by Fannie Flagg

# About the Author

Jacob Glass has been lecturing on spirituality since 1987. He resides in San Diego and Santa Barbara and is the founding minister of the 1st Church of Miracles. Audio tapes of his talks are ordered from all over the world.

If you would like to contact Jacob regarding his tapes, lectures or workshops:

(619)338-1646-email: Jaket36@aol.com

or on his website: http://members.aol.com/Jaket35/index.html

Made in the USA
Lexington, KY
27 October 2012